REVIEWS OF THE BOOK

"A remarkable story of a little girl's journey with God by her side the entire challenging way; most adults would have lost faith many, many times but not this child, young lady, and now an adult. She never even questioned her faith. God bless her."

—Bettye Rodgers

—⁊⁊—

"Brenda is an amazing woman of God. She is well-equipped to minister in this hour. Her book is truly evident of her God-given passion even as a young child growing up.

God has blessed Innovative Ministry, and she has been inspirational to so many.

She has ministered to the women in our church for several years now. We all look forward to receiving what God has given her.

We cherish the time she has allowed God to refresh, renew, and restore in her anointed sermons and workshops."

—First Lady Linda James Johnson Street CHSC

—⁊⁊—

Brenda,

I'm not even sure where to begin!

For one, I've never read a book this quick. Adrena Stephney could not put it down. I've cried, prayed, rejoiced, praised, and sometimes just stopped and quietly reflected upon the awesome God we serve. This book truly ministered to me. I loved the transparency. You poured your heart and soul into this work. The title is very fitting.

Not only is this your story, but your testimony. And can't nobody tell your testimony the way you can. They are subject to leave out the juicy part!

Throughout the reading, the Holy Spirit gave me songs for different chapters:

"For Every Mountain," "Lord Prepare Me (to be a Sanctuary),"

"Every Praise," "So Amazing," "Corinthian Song," and sometimes, it was just "Take Me to the King"!

Just give me Jesus! People are looking for something to hold onto or give them hope. This book definitely encouraged me to continue to run my race with great zeal. I know it will bless those whose hands and hearts receive it. You didn't tell me, it was a love story. I read a Love Story, and I mean a True Love Story. Someone who was truly in love with the Lover of her soul! There are just no words to explain or express your love for Audie.

Remarkable, unmatched, undying would be an understatement.

I thoroughly understand what you meant, when you said I had to function in "servant" and not "wife" mode. I can go on and on, but I am very grateful for the opportunity to be at this junction in life with you. I've always said, I will go to battle anytime, with somebody that is missing a limb or walk with a limp, etc. that tells me they have been through some things, but they've overcome them. Glory to God! I need somebody to get in the trenches, or go to battle with me if need be.

This book exudes the willful obedience of two servants that LOVE the Lord, and in spite of it all, have unspeakable Joy! Time after time, your heart was broken, your spirit was heavy, and your mind was confused–JOY rises up! But God. He put that in the inside of us, and hell can't shake it.

You made a choice to STOP looking for a miracle, and just BE one! All I can say is "THE King Has One More Move."

I love you with all my heart, soul, and gizzards.

—Adrena Stephney

HAD IT NOT BEEN
FOR THE LORD
ON HER SIDE

HAD IT NOT BEEN FOR THE LORD ON HER SIDE

BRENDA MURPHY

TATE PUBLISHING
AND ENTERPRISES, LLC

Published by Tate Publishing & Enterprises, LLC
127 E. Trade Center Terrace | Mustang, Oklahoma 73064 USA
1.888.361.9473 | www.tatepublishing.com

Tate Publishing is committed to excellence in the publishing industry. The company reflects the philosophy established by the founders, based on Psalm 68:11,
"The Lord gave the word and great was the company of those who published it."

Book design copyright © 2015 by Tate Publishing, LLC. All rights reserved.
Cover design by Jeffrey Doblados
Interior design by Caypeeline Casas

Published in the United States of America
ISBN: 978-1-68118-819-5
1. Religion / Christian Life / Devotional
2. Religion / Christian Life / Spiritual Growth
15.07.23

This book is being dedicated to a true warrior, friend, and brother in Christ Jesus, Deacon Robert Gaines who left us entirely too soon. Thank you for your tireless work, efforts, support, love, dedication, and prayers. Your time spent here on earth was absolutely priceless. You touched and blessed more lives than you will ever know. We miss you terribly here on earth, but we are so grateful for the opportunity to share our walk with a man with such integrity, fortitude, compassion, and godliness as you. Until we meet again…

Also, this book is especially dedicated to several people who have influenced my life greatly over the years. In a lot of ways, these individuals may never know the everlasting impact and blessings their personal journeys, insight, devotion, contribution, and genuine prayers have paved the way for me to reach such heights, levels, and pivotal moments in my personal journey with God.

Last but certainly not least; this book is dedicated to two very special nieces who are more like sisters than anything else. They are smart, strong, sensitive, tenacious, witty, assured, anointed, gifted, triumphant, and endeavoring. I draw strength from their journeys, along with their peaks and valleys.

They can take a life licking but are relentless in their spiritual ticking. They are motivated by what others may deem to be their defeat, and they are shrewd when it comes to maneuvering in daily business affairs; in other words, they both can get the job done effectively! I have watched them grow in years past from young women into phenomenal women and head of in some cases, their very own households over the years, and today I must say, I am proud to know them as family and to share in their journeys.

ACKNOWLEDGMENTS

I would like to personally thank my wonderful, amazing mother, Mrs. Frances Lovelace Little, for her outward devotion, dedication, relentless prayers, compassion, and unyielding faith that she provided to me through her everyday living. Through the devotion of her life to doing the will of God, she gave me hope, needed strength, and unlimited reasons to which I should always be thankful and to bless His name because He is worthy of the praise.

Frances lived her faith life out in the public view and was never ashamed to let others know where her faith lied and to whom she trusted. Because of her wisdom, tenacity to serve so boldly, I am assured today she is one of the primary reasons why I am endeavoring to serve God with such a passion and a relentless praise and devotion. Frances instilled in me the need for my personal walk with God, and for that, I am eternally grateful.

I would like to dedicate my thankfulness to a woman, who has since gone home to live eternally with her Lord and Savior, Mrs. Gertrude Moore, who was no doubt one of the greatest Sunday school instructors this side of heaven. This woman was nothing short of amazing. I would like to thank her for being the distinguished, incredible, wise, and prudent servant of God she was.

She served God with excellence. Her faith never wavered. She taught, lived, and breathed the life she taught her students about. Her work spoke for her. Her dedication to God allowed the world to see and those that knew her best to see that her living was not in vain. In her death, her legacy lives on to date; Thank you, Mrs. Moore, for leaving your spiritual light and legacy on for me and countless of others to follow.

To my brothers and sisters who have all played a very significant and specific role in my life, I want to take this opportunity to say thank you for all the life lessons learned.

When you didn't think that I was paying personal attention to your guidance, direction, suggestions, and even chastisements, I was in fact taking it all in.

Storing it all up for the future because I knew one day it would all come in handy. Thank you for all the personal life lessons learned through your trials, journeys, valleys, and triumphs. What you all did not know was that not only was I paying close attention, I was being inspired, intrigued, and motivated by your being my big brothers and sisters. Thank you for your love, brotherhood, and sisterhood over the many, many years. It has and still is very much appreciated.

CONTENTS

CHILDHOOD MEMORIES

I considered myself to be an ordinary child growing up in a loving home with parents who, like every other American family, just wanted the very best for their children. My parents believed in God; they worshiped God, and they took Him at His Word. They did so because they recognized that trying to raise a large family without God would have been too challenging otherwise.

By the time I was around the age of 10, I could readily sense the everyday struggles that my family faced just to make ends meet. Even though my parents did not always talk about the "lack" of things, the presence of it was always near. I could tell that my parents' most prized possessions and what they valued and appreciated the most was recognizing that God would ultimately see them through any situation.

Through their actions, my parents believed that since God had blessed them with such a large family, He alone would continue to watch over them even when facing any difficulties or problems along the way. My parents were both very proud yet humble of all of their children. There were no big I's and little You's.

During those very hard and lean times, when it seemed that my parents did not have enough money, food, or enough of anything, instead of crumbling under pressure, they knew how to rely upon God and to be of good cheer. They had witnessed God come through on many occasions, and each time He did, He was always on time.

When I was just a child, even then I noticed that God had blessed me and my siblings with loving, kind, and compassionate parents. To us, what our parents seemingly lacked in earthly possessions to give to us, God more than made up for it in favor, grace, and mercy.

Being blessed with five brothers and four sisters, we did not always grow up in the same environment. By the time I was in the eighth grade, my sister Vera had already moved out, leaving me with my two older brothers, Henry and Eddie, at home. However, that did not matter; I still heard enough about everyone else's lives to draw my own personal conclusions. Admittedly, most of them seemed intriguing at best.

From the very beginning, I didn't really get to explore what I would call a normal childhood. Oftentimes, I was challenged by various sicknesses that seemed to plague me for much of my childhood.

This caused me to miss a lot of days out of school as well as rendered me to be unable to attend both kindergarten and preschool like other children my age. Because of the sickness, I felt heavily guarded by both my parents and my siblings, who spent a lot of time looking after me before and after school. While I understood how they must have felt to some degree, I would have given anything not to be in that situation to begin with. For years, I struggled with medical issues even into first grade. There were days when I was healthy enough to attend school and some days, quite frankly, I was not. Nevertheless, I always considered myself to be a fighter and never gave up easily.

Sometimes I would be able to walk to the school bus and even ride all the way to school, before my illness would overtake me. At other times, I would be taken straight to the hospital where I would be given more medications rather than solutions regarding my illness.

Becoming very tired, weary, and discouraged from the wear and tear of it all, I often felt that the sickness and the fact that others had to take care of me was becoming too much not only for them, but others who appeared to be running out of patience with me and the sickness. I just wanted to run away and hide from it all.

Spending a lot of time alone in my room, I could often be found reading or coloring in my coloring book, playing with my doll house or tea set. Many days, I had to entertain myself because my other siblings were either out doing chores, homework, or just out playing with their friends.

Over the years, I learned how to entertain myself and thought literally nothing of it. In fact, for me, this was quickly becoming my new norm. Besides, kids my age would only tease me relentlessly and questioned why I walked funny, or talked funny or the fact that I didn't look or act like all the other children. Truly, I did not think that I was supposed to.

The cruelty of remarks other children and even the comment of my own siblings would make from time to time would make me feel like they did not care. At times, as a result of their comments, even as a child, I allowed those words to sometimes serve as stones to strip away my confidence, self-esteem and my desire to even try to move forward in my progress.

Even still, I pressed on. Growing up, I always admired my dad. I would often follow him out to the barn and watch him milk the cows and feed all the animals. I would ask him not to work too hard, and could be found saying "Okay, Dad, that's enough. Let's go to the house."

He would often think that it was funny and just pat me on the head. As I was growing up, the medical condition continued to challenge me. I felt as though I was not being cured but rather all the doctors did was kept me medicated as they continued guessing what the medical conditions were. Being extremely frightened and unable to verbalize my worst nightmare, I prayed constantly for change.

I found that outlet in my mother Frances, who not only prayed daily for me; but she was considered a prayer warrior in her own right. To me, Frances was considered my hero. Someone I grew to look up to. She was not only my mother but she was also someone I grew to admire, adore, and emulate.

For me, the sole purpose of me writing this book is to show the readers how important and real my walk in Christ was and still is for me today and that for me understanding that with God, all things were and are indeed possible. My hope is that the book will serve as a compass and encourager for other individuals who may feel as though they have missed God along the way and cannot return to their true love.

Early on, I did not always have confidence, strength, or insurmountable faith to move forward in my everyday decisions. There were times unfortunately; I allowed others to dictate some of my comings and goings. However, in my adult life, I have grown tremendously and I have gained a different perspective on what it means to be a daughter of the most high and walk in the call on my life.

Today, I have no doubt that I am a much stronger woman, a dedicated wife, caring and compassionate sister and a warrior of the Most High God. I choose to have the faith that I lacked in the past. And now, I embrace my life and believe that God has indeed created me for a purpose and a plan for my existence.

My desire is to share my experiences, dreams, joys, and triumphs with others to encourage and motivate them to move forward and to never look back or settle for anything less than what God has called, created, and birthed in them to do.

This book is written to express what my life was like growing up and starting my interesting journey. The intimate details and writings of this book are designed so that others will read it and glean from it God's supernatural ability to move on my behalf as well as open and close doors at His discretion for my life.

For me, I hope the book will foster a positive outlook on others' lives as well. It is so important for me that others know that God loves them and He delights in healing the brokenness in our lives and turning our lives around for betterment. I want the world to know that God is indeed a keeper even when the very last thing we may want or even feel that we need is to be kept.

To me, a little girl who was seemingly born into sickness, and surrounded by imperfections, I thought my mother's prayers and dedication to the Lord were amazing. Through my mother's prayers I learned that God was quicker than an instance and faster than real-time.

Daily, as my faith continued to be stretched, I came to realize that God was becoming a wonder in my soul through the personal signs of healing, endurance, strength, and wisdom. The more I trusted him, the more he continued to show me love and compassion for my life. Daily I tried to display my continuous witnessing of God's faithfulness in my life. The more I relinquished my life to the Lord, I saw my life changing for the better, and I wanted more of that drive every day.

As a result of that, my appetite became more insatiable for the Word of God and prayer. Through learning how to pray, I experienced God becoming more personable to me. I recognized and relied upon Him to be my healer, counselor, provider, and sustainer of all things.

I was learning how to cast all of my cares, fears, sickness, and doubts upon Him because I could feel that He genuinely cared for me. The closeness I felt while in His presence left no doubt in my mind that He alone could totally sustain me.

I was born and raised in a small town, with meager means at best. The house my family and I lived in was nothing short of basic shelter—basic being the operative word. Still my household, I felt, I had one of the most important ingredients necessary, and that was love and each other.

The house I grew up in was simple in shape—living room, three bedrooms and a study. I remembered the house having a long hallway with a big piano which we all tried to pretend that we knew how to play.

Our house had many interesting trinkets such as a big old cedar trunk, which I loved. It boasted of a cedar pine like smell. I absolutely loved it! If only I had known its true value and worth at the time, I would have never let it get out of my sight, especially as an adult. I thought to myself, when you don't know the value of something, there is a tendency to underestimate its worth and sometimes may end up paying a much higher price for it at a later time.

Additionally, our house was very interesting to say the least. Each room in the house had its own fireplace which made it very cozy. Lots of space to play, hide, pretend, and definitely get into trouble. It had lots of acreage complete with lakes and ponds to fish and swim. It also had a club house as well.

The house did not have any central air, water, or air conditioning, so everything was pretty much a chore and required a lot of work in maintaining its daily upkeep. If the family wanted water, we had to walk to the well to get it; but the water was absolutely fresh, cool, and very refreshing. It was definitely worth the walk, with fun and laughter on the way.

My siblings and I were silly kids who played together all the time. We could be found putting on fashion shows and family talent shows. We would play such games as hide-and-go-seek, redlight-green-light stop, and any other games we could think of.

No matter what, we were never ever bored.

Traditionally, during the summer, my two brothers, Henry and Eddie, would build me an annual playhouse in the backyard. On one occasion, to everyone's surprise, my nieces and nephew found an unlikely visitor waiting for us in the backyard one morning. It was one of the horses that had gotten out of the stables and took up refuge in the playhouse.

The problem was, after he had gotten into the play house, he was too large to get out. Now he was stuck with his head through the roof. As kids do, we screamed, laughed, cried, and even tried to bribe the horse who looked at us chewing on a packet of donuts as if to say, "Deuces, not today!"

As mentioned before, indeed the house was special. It was surrounded by ponds and lakes. It even had barns, numerous sheds a separate place for laundry, and a well that had the best water in the United States.

While the house did not have an inside house phone, it had a little booth for the telephone in the laundry room; just imagine, every time the telephone would ring, one of the siblings had to run and answer it. We used that as an exercise regimen!

Although the house was beautiful in its own way, there were a lot of things that made it difficult to live in as well. For starters, in the winter, there was no central heat, so my dad and brothers would have to go outside and chop wood and bring it back to the house to make fires every day. While the fire burned, everything was perfect; however, when it went out, it could get cold very quickly. We didn't have running water in the house, so we often had to plan a schedule as to who would do what chore on each day.

I grew up on a farm with parents who rarely bought anything from the grocery store. They did not need to since they grew all their vegetables fresh from the garden. We gathered milk, eggs daily from the hen house, and fish from the pond.

Our mother made sure that everyone had chores and then some. And to make sure that everyone was clear, she made a list for each child and placed it where we could all easily find it. Trust me, those chores on that list had "better" be done by the time she returned home and if they were not, there would be major consequences to pay… and all of my brothers and sisters reading this book would say, "Amen."

Our family was like all other red-blooded American families. We could always be found bickering, getting into fights, and doing our own thing when Mom and Dad were nowhere around. Henry, the oldest of the boys at home, loved to fish and was extremely good at it.

He loved to hunt, which was his second passion. He was equally talented at it as well. Eddie, in my opinion, was well-rounded and could do anything he put his mind to. He was more self-sufficient than Henry because he always stayed focused on the matter at hand, and he didn't require too much attention.

Vera was the only sister at home at the time, and I so admired her. To me, Vera was a second hero. I never told her that in so many words, but she was and still remains so. I thought Vera was the smartest, prettiest girl on the planet. Vera absolutely loved to read her Harlequin romance novels, cook, and decorate; and she was great at them all. To me, Vera was one of the most thoughtful, humble, and intelligent person I know. Growing up, I learned a lot from my big sister. Most importantly, I learned very quickly never ever attempt to come between Vera and her soaps or her Harlequin romance, or you face the wrath!

Growing up, I can remember our mother being a little fireball for Jesus. She was not afraid to "Let her little light shine!" For some, it infuriated them because apparently they had allowed their lights to become dim or had already considered themselves all flickered out! My mother was my role model because she demonstrated Christ likeness everyday through her living and giving to both family first and then to others. My mother encouraged me to pray early in life and to always put God first and to trust Him with my whole heart.

Little did I know then that the God that I so openly talked so boldly about would one day become my everything. No ifs, ands, or buts. Today, my relationship with Jesus is to me what oxygen is to every living being. It's a necessity to live.

My mother's lifestyle exemplified Christ in all that she did, touched, and displaced. She was hardworking, sincere, fierce, and a force to be reckoned with. She was funny, talented, gifted, true, honest, caring, and trustworthy. When she loved, she loved with her whole heart. When she gave, she provided wisdom and insight in her giving. She gave without keeping score; she gave in abundance without expectation of others to give back to her. She gave without guilt and because of that I truly believed that God gave her more in the end.

I truly believed that there were those who disliked my mother because she was a giver and one who appreciated and understood the art of giving than receiving. My mom understood the phrase in Philippians that said, "*In everything I did, I showed you that by this kind of hard work we must help the weak, remembering the words the Lord Jesus himself said: 'It is more blessed to give than to receive'*" (Acts 20:35, NKJV).

My mother was always saying things like, "Baby, put God first," "It's better to give than to receive." Really, Mom, at that time, I could not understand that concept but I would not dare ask her that question out loud. How I longed to someday be that close to God as well.

My mother was well aware of how much God loved her and that He loved her for who she was in the body of Christ. She readily acknowledged His presence in her life. She daily thanked him openly for his grace and mercy towards her and her family.

My mother served out of her weaknesses and her strength. To me, when my mother "worshipped" God, you could literally feel the residue from her worship to Him. She calls it the overflow of the spirit of God. She served him with her whole heart. She didn't leave any stone unturned. She served God with infectious gladness and deliberate awareness. She served without withdrawal! All the while, others whispered, snickered, and gossiped, "Does it really take all that to praise him?" "I wonder what she is going through." My mom remained focused and true while others were judging her by her outer circumstances and saying things like: "Poor thing, she had all those children, how is she going to make it?" I witnessed my mother always relying upon God to see her through. When others in the family saw lack of food for example, our mother only saw an opportunity for God to provide and do His perfect work.

Throughout Frances's life, I witnessed my mother grow comfortable being under the shadows of the wings of the Almighty God. Up until her death, Frances was a woman of substance with a clear and precise vision of whom she served.

Whether it was public or private, everyone knew that she loved God because of her walk and faith in Him. Frances's family, friends, and those that she deemed important to her meant the absolute world to her. Her earthly family was always first. She was a good wife, mother, nurturer, caregiver, provider, friend, and servant of the God Most High.

Her children were probably one of her greatest accomplishments in the entire world. She loved all of us equally. Each of her children had a piece of her heart, no doubt about it. Every chance she got, she told us by saying, "Momma love all of her children." And she adamantly challenged us to "love ye one another."

Our mother was often criticized even within her own family for not loving each of her children equally even though, there was not one that she adored more than the other. Sure she may have doted on one more than the other at times, but that was because she deemed that child needed her more. Now, just because she did that does not mean that the other siblings saw it the same way through their eyes, or understood it for that matter. However, that's how mom chose to handled it.

I would be the first to say, that it is quite difficult to judge a book by its cover if you really haven't taken the time to at least explore the pages and its contents first. In my mind, it is easy to judge another mother when the persons judging is not standing in that individual's shoes nor experiencing what that individual may be going through at the time.

Nevertheless, mom loved each of her children unconditionally and she thoroughly enjoyed making a difference in our lives. She would not allow anyone to tell her how to raise and love her children. Not even her other children, friends, family members, or foes. She loved us all equally.

My dad (Jake) was mild-mannered. He thoroughly enjoyed life, love, and laughter. He truly enjoyed his family, especially his sons. He didn't slight his daughters, but one could tell that his sons were precious to him. My dad enjoyed the presence, time and attention his sons spent with him going fishing, hunting, and chopping wood together.

Our dad was considered a jokester at best. Not only did he enjoy telling stories, he would laugh at himself while doing so inevitably, causing everyone else around him to laugh as well. Our dad cared about making sure people saw the big picture in life and not getting hung up on trivial things.

He was not overly concerned with things that were unimportant. He cared more about people knowing that he loved them and wanted the best for them. Our dad was also a great listener and the kind of man that was quick to hear and very slow to respond.

His behavior caused some people great anguish and dislike towards him. Even still, our dad still remained true to his belief. He remained focused, calm, cool, and always collected.

He listened with great anticipation as if he wanted to make sure that his response to that individual he was advising was what God wanted him to say—nothing more and nothing less.

Our dad was about building others up not tearing people down. He lived his life as an encourager and not a hinderer of other individual's progress. In my opinion, he was a mentor and driver of sorts always providing a glimmer of hope and life to any dead situation.

In a lot of ways, I considered my Dad as being my mentor because he often spoke truth even if it was not readily received by others. Although dad did not graduate from high school or attend college, however, he was a wonderful provider for his family and a great man of standard. He loved life and treasured his family above all other earthly possessions.

Dad was kind, gentle, harmless, and easy to love. He too loved God and often sought His will for his life and that of his family. He cared about those around him. Dad often spoke things in a parable manner. For instance, he would say things like, Baby, nothing comes to a sleeper but a dream" or "A man that doesn't work should expect not to eat."

My parents were successful because they prayed for and with each other continuously. They stood together and on one accord believing God for the same expected end.

Out of a family of nine children, I was blessed with four very strong, feisty, independent, intelligent, smart, and sometimes headstrong sisters. I grew tremendously being in their shadow and admiring them all from afar. At the time, I also had five older brothers who were and still are equally giving and loving in their own ways.

My siblings and I were no different than any other family. Like other families, we had our share of arguments, disagree sibling rivalry, and even a bit of jealousy, strife, and occasional name calling. You know all the fun stuff true family members are really made of.

CURIOSITIES GOT THE BEST OF ME

My childhood in my opinion was full of questions and curiosity. I spent a lot of time day-dreaming about my future. Even as a kid, I always knew that I would do great exploits in my life for the kingdom of God. Honestly, in my world, I never thought of anything else I would rather do. Even when I was very young, all I ever truly wanted to do was to take the kingdom of God by storm and tell others about the great God that I served.

In the early stages of my youth, and even through my sickness, I learned to lean and to depend upon God for everything, especially as my healer. I realized that when I prayed to God, there was a sense of closeness and oneness that I had never experienced and I definitely wanted more of that at all times.

As my relationship with the Lord grew, I learned to depend upon Him more. I would often day dream about what heaven was like. What the angels must look like. I was convinced that I had a one-on-one direct connection with God because whenever I spent precious time away just to be alone with him, His divine presence showed up each and every time to meet with me.

He never once let me down. Daily I set aside personal time to talk with him. I would often cry out to him about my problems, sickness, direction, and just the plans he had for my life. My conversations with God were not what someone might call "prayers" in a traditional way; but rather, just daily communication I called it where two people share thoughts, concerns, cares, highlights and even low points of their lives.

I didn't necessarily see God as being a Father far away in heaven, but a very special and close friend that was always near me and being accessible to me whenever I needed Him the most. Spending countless hours throughout my day talking to God and growing closer to Him, I asked Him one day during prayer to "either please heal my body or to allow me to come home to be with Him" being tired of being sick, I wanted His presence more.

Although this statement might seem extreme to others, this was the type of relationship I had with God that I felt I could ask him anything and He would listen. Perhaps my reasoning for making such a bold statement was that I believed my personal acceptance of Christ into my life would allow me entrance into His kingdom and going home to be with my Lord and Savior was the best thing that could possibly ever happen to me even at such a young age.

From what I had read, there would be no more sickness, death, hurt, pain, sadness and I thought compared to all the pain and daily medical issues I was continuously experiencing at that time, what better place to be than at home in the presence of my Lord and Savior.

Whenever I saw progress in my life, I took that as a sign that God heard me and was moving on my behalf. There was no doubt that He loved me. I had a great presence of God in my life. I was mindful of His anointing in my life, although I did not relate to the closeness as an "anointing" but more or less a close presence instead. All I knew and understood was that He was real and that He truly cared for me and that was all I needed.

Realizing that the doctors were doing the best they could with the knowledge they had, I knew if I were to be healed and had any possible real chance of survival it would only come through the sheer will of God. With the desire to live what I called a "normal" life, I turned my life over to the Lord and let him have His own way in and through it.

I was becoming relaxed in my relationship in God. I never doubted His instructions. In fact, I heard them clearly and precisely. Not knowing any differently, I assumed that everyone heard and responded the same way. The more God showed up in my life, the more I surrendered my all to Him.

Because I was always fascinated about nature and what made things evolve and work, I would take long walks whenever permitted. Often I could be found sitting out in the pastures, swaying in the wind among the wild flowers. I figured that if the flowers could praise God, surely I could, and I was not one to be outdone.

I would sway in the wind and sing my favorite songs, from "My Soul Loves Jesus" and "Yes Jesus Loves Me." Oftentimes when I was praising God, tears would stream inevitably down my cheeks; this is when I felt the closest to Him. I felt as though He was holding me ever so close to His side.

The real truth of the matter was the closer I grew to the Lord, I began keeping a journal, asking why this and why that. I would bug anyone that would listen to me about their thoughts on following Jesus. I loved Him just that much and I could make a sermon out of a bologna sandwich if only time permitted.

For me this was considered as normal behavior and that everyone acted this same way. I never saw myself as being odd or strange when it came to praise and worship in any way. Daily I yearned to spend more quite time with God and often used any excuse to do so. I wanted to learn and experience more and more about Him. I was simply intrigued and driven to know more.

Even with great role models and a God whom I believed loved me, there was nothing about my life that was ever really easy. For me, each day was set into survival mode especially over my thought life.

During my early years, I was sickly at lot. At times I found it difficult due to severe pain and stiffness in my legs to walk and to do much of anything other kids got a chance to do like run and play outside. When this happened to me, I would have to sit and rest for long periods of time in order to regain my strength.

Not only was this a very painful and uncomfortable situation for me, there were many kids who made fun of my situation which also caused me pain and sadness. There were times in my life I would experience severe chest pains which caused shortness of breath. During those episodes, I would wonder if the next would indeed be my last.

When these episodes would occur, I was always thankful that my mother was around. For some reason, her face and prayers always comforted and calmed me and in a lot of ways, they kept me hopeful that I would survive another day.

Days, weeks, months, and even years passed by when my mom would take me from doctor appointments to doctor appointments and all I ever received from those visits were more medications and a guesstimate about what my diagnosis would be. I hated every moment of it. In the grand scheme of things, I began to pray to God more and more about my condition.

While I had not openly acknowledged God as being Lord of my life, I knew that He was able because daily I had personal experience of his faithfulness to me. In His presence, the sickness seemed to simply melt. I often witnessed him working in the life of my mom as well.

I would often sense the very presence of God through my mother's prayers and testimonies. When she would pray over me, I instantly gained strength and a renewed sense to forge forward no matter what. I knew I had a resolve deep within me to live and not die.

During my early years, I was painfully shy. Often I endured a lot of criticism and taunting from others. At times, this caused me to question my confidence about how I genuinely processed and internalized certain things.

After much negativity in my life, I rarely trusted anyone to openly talk to about my emotions, situation, and experiences.

Even though I wanted real friends in my life, I was too afraid to open up and trust others.

People often felt the need to fill in the blanks for my life. Never taking the time out to listen or to truly see me, they assumed they already knew everything about me, and for that, they already had a preconceived notion of how to respond to my concerns even before I would ask any questions.

What I personally discovered was that the world and no doubt others in my life were looking for someone they deemed normal and to them; I was anything but according to them. I had a sickness no one knew what to call and I struggled to keep up with the other children my age in school.

When it became painfully clear that no one wanted to accept me into their circle of friends, I resolved to be a loaner which was not entirely bad. I spent a lot of time entertaining myself by reading, coloring, and playing with my tea set. Interesting enough, my favorite book became the Kings James Version of the Bible.

In fact, I found myself being intrigued by it the more I read and discovered the various scriptures and teachings about Jesus and His power. Daily, I was growing by leaps and bounds spiritually. As my reading and studying of the bible intensified, I chose to steal away more often and talk to God above everything that concerned me. Doing so, I began to build a personal relationship with Him. I often confided in God about daily concerns. Talking to God automatically put my mind at ease and just taught me that everything was going to be okay.

Daily I would pour my heart out to Him without feeling overwhelmed or feeling guilty with the consequences of it all. For some reason I felt at home with Him. Comfortable with His presence as if we had been friends for years; I felt that He knew my every move and that He cared.

I knew He cared about me and my situation; even though I really didn't understand it, His presence kept drawing me closer and closer to Him and I eagerly accepted His divine invitation. The more I sought His presence, the more His presence put me at ease and I seemed more and more intrigued by it all.

ENTERING INTO HIS DAILY PRESENCE

I absolutely liked the way I felt when I was drawn into the presence of God. Whenever I entered into His presence, I immediately felt as if I belonged and that I was loved. There was a sense of contentment, and that I was surrounded by something or someone much greater, capable, and able than myself.

While sitting before Him, I was constantly reminded that there was no need of fear, doubt, shame, or embarrassment. I truly felt protected in every sense of the word, and I genuinely longed for more time alone with Him.

As time passed, I began to thoroughly enjoy my quite time alone imagining my life from the various stories in the Bible. While reading, I would get so caught up in the moment, I would not notice if someone was watching me or not. Truth being told, during those times, I never felt freer than I ever had in my entire life.

While other kids were probably reading their favorite books like Jack in the Beanstalk or The Three Little Pigs, I was busy enjoying books like Ezekiel, John, Matthew, Luke, and Hebrews. Bless my heart I would do just about anything to be alone with my Bible because it became my best friend and my source for living.

After a while, it didn't seem like I was reading a bunch of words or just another book. Rather, I found myself being fully engaged in a meaningful conversation daily with my new found friend and confidante.

I looked forward to our agreed upon time to meet. By now I could not wait to be alone with my new found friend so that I could share my heart and dreams with. I felt that He literally understood everything about me.

Over time, I began to crave and desire His presence more than being with others. I would skip dinner and pretend to be sleepy or sick just to be alone with God. I enjoyed talking with him even though I really didn't know if what I was asking was considered as right or wrong; all I knew was that I wanted more of His presence.

My desire for the Word was becoming more insatiable. My thirst for wisdom and knowledge was important to me and longing to be in His presence became the greatest focus of my day. As I anticipated what He would say to me through His word, and I was always in awe of Him.

I was attracted to the support and emotional stability I felt when I was near His presence. I felt that each time I called the name of God, even through a whisper, He was absolutely listening to me and attentive to my every cry.

I loved God because I could count on Him to be there without fail. I could rest in Him with my whole being. I believed that He was there for me no matter what. The evidence proved it every time. Whenever I was aware that He was near me, I no longer felt alone or lonely. I didn't feel drained as I had been before. The frustrations weren't there; I felt that it was going to be alright. I felt guarded, protected, and cared for by someone greater who loved me and only wanted the best for me.

Even as a child, I knew the difference. It was like night and day. Right and wrong, truth and fiction; there is a genuineness when you are in the presence of the Almighty God. There are no pretenses. No fakeness. No hidden agenda. Even though it cannot be explained, there is a sense that there is something much greater than yourself around.

There in the presence of God, I describe my time as being a sense of oneness and vulnerability. I had never witnessed such peace and utter calmness in my life. Slowly but surely my personal conversations with God was becoming priority over my thoughts and my personal life. I felt that I was being taught personally about him in private classes.

During our time together, I felt that I was definitely in a class of one. Even though I was young, I found myself longing for the Word of God more and more. Absolutely nothing else in my life really mattered more than my private time alone with the Almighty God.

When I read the Word of God I would feel anew. I felt revived and rejuvenated, and in that moment, very much alive and well. No pain inflicted my body. I felt whole, purposed, and defined. I felt that I belonged to something much greater than myself, and therefore, it became easier for me to yield while in His presence. No fear! As crazy as this may sound to some, I truly believed that I heard him speak to me often through a thought, the wind, or a familiar song during intimate prayer time we spent together.

One of my favorite books of the Bible to this day, is the book of Ezekiel. One of my favorite passages of scripture reference is 37:1–10, The Dry Bones Live. I could relate to this passage the most because of the pain and aches within my own body and with all of my sicknesses and temporary disabilities; I felt I could definitely relate to being so disconnected from everything and sometimes everybody.

I felt dismantled from the world, even at times, from my family as though I didn't belong and as if I were a misfit living in society. But when I encountered the presence of God, all I needed to do was just enter in and immediately, I felt accepted by Him.

All along, I had no earthly idea that this presence with God was molding me and shaping me into the image that God wanted me to be. I dreamed that one day I would be used mightily by

God to speak to the masses about His greatness, and that one day, I would be used by Him for His glory.

What I knew for sure was even when I fell in what seemed to be unbearable, unreachable, and impossible situations in my personal life, God seemed to always know where I was ahead of time, how I arrived there, and just how long I would remain in that specific situation. Even though I didn't know how I was going to escape, He always provided a way of escape for me.

No matter what hardship or situation I found myself in, God never left me alone. He always provided a way of greater escape sooner rather than later. As I continued to pursue the Word of God, it was becoming crystal clear to me that my appetite for God's Word was becoming intense.

I found myself daydreaming about the Word of God, imagining myself teaching before people, even though at the time, I was afraid of my own shadow. Anxiously waiting to read the next chapter in the Bible, I looked forward to talking to God wondering what He had to say to me the next time we met in our "private chat room."

I never worried about life with God beyond this moment, because to me, this was just between the two of us and no one else needed to know or would ever know. It was, after all, what I called and considered to be a private conversation that continued to grow and expand between myself and God. It was working for me. By now, I was considering this presence as my "friend," and daily I welcomed Him in with open arms.

Back to my mother, she always took church and the things of church extremely seriously. She never liked for the children to "play" church, which is one of my favorite things to do growing up. I loved to gather everyone together and "pretend" we were in church.

I was the pastor or the teacher for that Sunday. I thoroughly enjoyed expressing and sharing the Word of God to all who would diligently listened. I can just about imagine what my family and friends thought of me. They believed I was beyond my years…

Even that didn't stop me. I was too much involved. I had to have more of Him and nothing and no one was going to interfere in my reaching my personal and private goal. Just the mentioning of the name of God would literally light up my being. I would become enameled with everything that gave me hope. Somehow, the Word of God consistently drew me in without effort. From the very inception of reading, I was smitten to say the least. There was no turning back, no way!

What I would later learn was that everyone else would not necessarily share my excitement about my relationship with Christ. In fact, there were many who thought that I was even stranger and abnormal because I did, and they were not always shy in letting me know that either.

Talk about your feeling being hurt, that wasn't even the half of it. Anything from name calling to downright being mean is just some of the things I personally had to endure as time passed. I honestly thought that loving God and demonstrating His love to others was the way that "all church" people felt since that's what people talked about on Sundays and Wednesday nights at bible study. Let's just say I was severely wrong.

My peers did not want anything to do with me. Every chance they got, they avoided me like the plague. Not being accepted by my peers bothered me considerably; even still, I was not willing nor could I change the course of my life just to please others.

During my earlier years, I endured my share of disappointments, setbacks, and even setups. I was often overlooked even when I was an asset to the team. At times, I was told that no one would truly love me or that I would never truly be accepted because of my love for God.

One could only imagine what this type of behavior and words did for my self-esteem. Daily I questioned my own abilities. I was slowly learning that had it not been for God on my side, I would never make it alone. I needed the constant reassurance from Him that I would be okay; and I could honestly say, every time I asked for His guidance, I received it sometimes in double dosages.

When I was being tested by some people who were supposed to love me and not harm me, it caused me to become bitter and sometimes critical in my thinking of those individuals. My tone of voice and responses could some days be viewed as brash or harsh. To them perhaps, they saw me as being mean; I saw it as a means to survival from the wolves that seemingly lied in wait for my soul. For me, I fought back by any means I could.

Despite what people were saying about me and how they mistreated me, I was learning through the Word of God that I was more than a conqueror and that I possessed a warrior's spirit within myself and even in the midst of it all, I remembered still having enough presence about myself to continue to call upon the Name of God to move forward.

When I called Him, I did so with all of my heart and broken-ness. I cried out to and for Him to help me because I realized I did not possess the inner strength to live on my own without being incubated by His Holy Spirit. When I cried out for help, immediately assistance was dispatched without fail, and it was always on time.

As the months turned into years, God became my personal confidante, protector, friend, victor, and most especially, my healer. Yes, my healer. I felt there was nothing I could not share with Him about my life. Every chance I had, I called upon the name of Jesus without fully understanding that His name would later be known to me as the name that was above every name. I hadn't made it that far yet in my personal relationship with Him. I just knew that what I was searching for was more than what I could handle at the time.

One day, while hiding out in one of my many locations and talking with God, I forgot to secure the lock on the door; and when I came to myself while having "church," I discovered that my mother was standing in the doorway. I just knew that this was the beginning of the end of my friendship with God because my mother did not play church—although I was not playing. I didn't know if my mother fully understood, and I was too afraid to try and explain.

No life flashing before my eyes, no sweet music, no program, or anything just stillness. The kind where you only hear the birds chirping! Oh God, I said if there was ever a time for delivering me up, now would be good.

When I could swallow and gather my bearings about myself, I asked my mother how long had she been standing there? Her reply was, "Never mind that. How long have you being doing this?"

When I opened my mouth to try to respond, tears immediately rolled down my face, and I blurted out, "Momma, I am not playing church. I am just talking to God." Surprisingly, my mother's reply was, "Baby, I know you are not playing church, but how long have you been doing this?"

To that, I replied, "For a long time, I didn't want anyone to know." Both me and my mother hugged and cried, and my mother told me that I did not need to pretend anymore.

No one could imagine just how freeing that conversation must have been for me. From that day forward, I began to grow and explore more possibilities. Later that year, revival also began during the last week in July, and baptism was on the second Sunday in August. I was destined to "join" church that year, and I had already begun telling others that I was going to do just that "get saved."

Revival began in July, and even though it was hot and muggy, there was still a sense of sweet savory in the atmosphere and a sense of change and a birthing of something new on the horizon in my young life. I eagerly asked my mother if I could join the other kids my age during revival, and my mother responded, "Only if you're sincere."

Well, that was only music to my ears. My reply was, "Of course, yes, yes and yes." My parents took revivals and anything that had to do with church seriously. During revival time, I could not have friends over, watch television, and chat on the phone or any distractions at all.

My entire focus was on praying and seeking God. Well, for me, that was until my favorite soap operas came on, which were *The Young and the Restless* and *As the World Turns*. Come on, who didn't watch that? Nevertheless when those shows came on, I began to focus more of my attention on my soaps rather than praying. I mean it was only for a couple of hours, right?

Consequently, rather than spending quality time in private prayer as promised. I could not wait to share the soap opera information with my mom well, let's just say it didn't quite go over too well. My mother strongly suggested to me to wait until the next year until I was a little more mature before entering into revival. I agreed with my mom and sadly complied with her wishes.

While anticipating what the next year would bring, I continued my daily quest to become closer to God. I could not wait to spend time reading and what I called talking with God each day. I didn't think of it as prayer as much as I did having a daily conversation with someone I cared so deeply about.

As the weeks turned into months, and months turned into the next year, there were many exciting and adventurous things that took place in the interim. Because I didn't deal well with storms, whenever there was one, I would run, hide, and pray with everything I had! I made all kinds of promises, such as "God, if you don't let the lights go out, I promise to get saved. If you just let the storm pass, I promise to be good for a whole week"

Needless to say during that year, I won some of the battles, and I lost most of them, not necessarily due to my fault. One particular night, the storm was raging, as my friends on The Little House on The Prairie would say, and my wonderful brother Henry, the jokester of the family, decided that he would once again scare the living daylights out of me and tell one of his made-up, scariest stories about ghosts and people returning back from the dead. Of all the nights, the lighting was flickering profusely, and the thunder clouds were extremely loud. And wouldn't you know it, everyone in the house was snoring and asleep but me and God. I literally cried and begged for mercy for Henry to stop telling the stories, but of course he wouldn't give in. That would be too much like right!

In fact, it actually made his night to scare his little sister to no end. During this horrific time, I cried to God and made all kinds of promises, even going so far as to plead with him to not allow the lights to go out because I was absolutely terrified of being in the dark. I couldn't tell you if the lights went out or not because I evidently cried myself to sleep to escape the madness of my looney brother Henry's crazy idea of a joke. Little did he know, I vowed to one day pay him back for all the misery and insane things he had enjoyed terrorizing me.

To me, that was the best way to begin a day. The first words out of my mouth were, "Thank you Lord for small but necessary favors" as I sprinted from my bedroom to a brand new day.

During the summer my mom and dad made sure that the kids were never bored around the house. Not even for one second. They always had enough chores to keep us extremely busy for two summers. Trust me; I was always assigned to the kitchen duties. I had enough dishes to wash to keep me busy from eighth grade to twelfth, I literally hated ever moment of it. As the months were progressing to July, the church annual revival began and I really never gave much thought about my previous promises that were made, although I was sincere at the time.

One day, while taking a nap in the afternoon on the sofa, I thought I was dreaming when I suddenly remembered hearing a plane flying above my house. In the dream, I could also visualize the plane flying on a beautiful day in the sky.

While hearing and sensing the plane, I could also sense that somehow, the plane was suddenly in trouble and beginning to descend right over my family's house. Honestly, I thought that it was going to crash right into it. It seemed as though I couldn't move no matter how hard I tried, and I became scared and braced myself for the inevitable.

Our house had a tin roof, and the noises from the plane over the house made the noise even more excruciatingly unbearable. Thinking I was going to die should the plane actually crash into the house, I began screaming and praying, "God help me, help me please." I felt paralyzed. I literally could not move. I felt helpless and frightened. Tried as I might, I could not seem to wake myself from the vision. The lower the plane got, the more worried and afraid I became because I thought it was going to crash into the house.

Thinking that this was it for me, I just simply yielded, when all of a sudden; I heard this voice above me, vividly saying, with a very pronounced tone, "Remember your promise, your promise, your promise" in an echo-effect tone.

Instantly, I was released from the previous hold I felt that I was in. I sat straight up on the couch, sweating and looking around to see if there was someone else in the room with me. Thankfully, there wasn't, but I couldn't immediately figure out what just happened or the particular feeling I had at the moment.

Terrified, I immediately went to find my mom and share the story. However, on the way there, I thought, how am I going to share this with my mom when I don't know or understand the purpose of it? All I knew was that it was profound and that I needed help in understanding what just happened to me. By the time I reached the kitchen, my mother was cooking when I asked, "Did you call me?"

"No," she replied. "Did you hear anything strange just a few minutes ago?" No, once again. Puzzled and still frightened, I attempted to try an explain to my mother what just happened to me but thought better of it and turned to walk out when my mother, whose back was turned to me asked, did you make any promises?

Well, I thought sure, but like everyone else in the moment, while the storm was raging, I was definitely sincere about the prayer request; however, after the storm was over, I simply forgot about it and moved on. Sounds familiar? When my mother asked that question, I immediately remembered making a very specific promise to God, and I said to my Mom, "Well, yeah but…" Mom replied, "Child, there's no buts about it. Either you did or you did not.

Remember the promise that I made was the commitment of getting saved that year. Revival was gearing up within two weeks, and I was very excited and nervous. I could not wait for the first day kickoff, because I enjoyed the excitement of others being excited about revival, singing, praising, and the preached word.

For me, the preached word was like music to my ears and my soul. It was just something magical about it. Whenever I was around, preaching, I would immediately feel engulfed by it— almost like being pulled away into another dimension and at peace. I absolutely loved to hear it. It was like angelical music to my being. Every time I "heard" it, I felt compelled to draw nearer to God.

Monday night was the kickoff night for revival my heart felt like it was racing out of my body. I felt this is it I was overjoyed. It was me and about five other individuals who sat on what was called at that time the "mourners' bench." While some people today would laugh one to scorn about this process, I personally would not trade this part of my personal journey for anything. It kept me focused and disciplined in all the right areas of my life. Today, this is why I believe that my life with the Lord is so vibrant because I learned how to spend time alone with him in my younger years.

To me, being set aside for such a time as this was special and specific. It helped me to get a proper prospective of my purpose for being. It was a very humbling experience. It was personal and intimate, and nothing else mattered in that moment but me and God. During this time, there was also someone being assigned to each individual, praying and interceding with all those who participated during the entire process.

Not even two days into revival, I felt differently, changed from the inside out. I knew that when I called upon the name of God, He would show up and so He did, and instantly, that same familiar presence was right there by my side all the way.

The more I prayed, the more I could feel His presence there with me; but now there was no escaping my emotions because they would be displayed in the public's view. This was new uncharted territory for me, so then I prayed, "Lord, if you are going to save me, please let me be in total control. I don't want to be like my grandmother, shouting and wailing and throwing my arms up in the air!"

Those who thought they knew me and had previously witnessed me praise the Lord did not know that they would be in for a new level of my love for Christ after I became saved. Every time I thought of His name and the goodness He had brought into my life, I just beamed with excitement and thanksgiving.

In that moment, all I could remember was just praise him. My mind was filled with praises; my gratitude was off the chart. I was amazed and felt amazing. During the second night of revival while in prayer, there were two twin sisters that were assigned to me as my intercessors; and when those two ladies prayed for me, they encouraged and motivated me all at the same time. I felt that I was blessed and fortunate to have them by my side. That night, there was no doubt that God had already saved me.

There was no doubt in my mind and in my soul. The earth seemed to shift, and I felt a shifting in my spirit that all was indeed well. However, I just wanted to be in control of my emotions. I remembered all too well what it was like praising God out in the pastures and the fields or on those long private walks to the mailbox to gather the mail. I knew what it was like to run in the spirit and shout when the greatness of God began to carry me out in the spirit realm and all I could feel surrounding me was His goodness and His mercy.

I remembered many private moments of crying and lying out before the Lord and asking him to help me, and He came quickly to my rescue. He became a hedge of protection around me, a bridge over the troubled waters, a shield, and a wheel in the middle of the wheel for me. In my heart, I just felt like saying hallelujah and thank you, Jesus!

Still, I didn't want people to laugh at me in the way I would do my dance before the Lord or how I would be found often lifting up my hands and singing before him. I could be found worshipping my God without a moment's notice or praising Him for how He was my healer. I believed that the adults would understand, but not my silly peers. After a while, I yielded my entire being unto God, and He indeed saved me that night and welcomed me into His kingdom!

Suddenly, my life had been changed for the better in an instant. There was absolutely no doubt or confusion in my mind. I had been officially changed. My being felt very much alive; my vision and perception were different. I was instantly filled with incredible joy and laughter. I was saved, delivered, and liberated.

In high school, I was unpopular with other girls because I never tried to fit in like all the rest. I was quiet and confident, always wanting to please the teachers and get good grades. While others just merely wanted to get by and be popular at someone else's expense.

This made others upset as a result. At times, I was misunderstood by my peers. They would laugh at me and call me names and said that I acted too old to be around them.

They mocked me for always attending church and praying with others. They would call me "holy roller" and "church girl." Even at a young age, I was always overlooked for games and sports but was the first one sought after for prayer, instruction, guidance, and reliance when they were in trouble. Isn't that something?

In my early years, I was often horrified at some of the names I was called, and how I was treated and mishandled by some of the students who never associated themselves with me. They hated me without even getting to know me on any level at all. Day after day, I would consistently endure backbiting, gossiping, cursing, and in general, just mean-spirited individuals with no consciousness at all. In fact, the more they badgered me, the more at ease in the presence of God I became.

You see, I knew how to rest in the Lord. I knew how to depend upon the Lord for my safety. I remember the scripture in Psalm 46:1 (KJV) that states, "*God is our refuge and strength, a very present help in times of trouble.*" It was important to note that if I didn't know anything else, I knew how to rely upon God and wait on him to make everything all right. I realized that this information only came through leaning and trusting in the Almighty one day at a time.

To say that I was offended, hurt, bruised, and even frightened by the treatment I received would be a gross understatement. There were many days when I did not want to leave my house, let alone attend classes. I never told anyone; I merely kept it all to myself, afraid, and more importantly, ashamed for anyone to find out how I was being bullied and hated. This may sound strange to most people, but I prayed a lot for God's protection in the midst of it all. I seriously sought God's protection over my life day and night without fail mainly because I felt He alone would understand and was able to help me even in this cruelty.

It shouldn't be shocking to anyone how this sort of treatment can wreak havoc upon anyone's life, sometimes even for the rest of their lives. At the very least, it caused me to question myself a lot and tore a hole temporarily in my self-confidence. But for the grace and sheer mercy of God, I never would have made it through.

I called on God even the more to just make it from day to day. I felt that I had no one else to turn to, not even my family in some instances because they all were very young and living their own lives. The last thing they wanted to be saddled with was a little sister with medical issues and self-esteem problems. The pain and hurt was often overwhelming to bear most days. Something deep down within me caused me to live and not die, not naturally speaking but spiritually so.

Even when I was out among friends, the only time I really ever felt comfortable was when I was alone reading, writing, or just talking to God. He became more and more precious to me. Just the mentioning of His name soothed me. His presence calmed me and steadied my very footsteps. In His presence I felt saved, protected, covered and not judged, and certainly not rejected.

While in His presence, even when I didn't know which way to turn, the Holy Spirit would instantly guide me into the right path. Since I had been changed, indeed old things were in fact passing away and new things were on the horizon for me. Thank you, Jesus!

THE PERSONAL JOURNEY BEGINS

Eventually, I graduated from high school and thought that my life would get better as far as how others would accept me for who and how I was. Well, was I ever surprised? Even moving away from home didn't prevent the enemy from trying to take me out—discrediting my name, integrity, hope, peace, and certainly my identity in Christ. After moving away from home, I still continued to endure even more daily criticism. I never felt so misunderstood, overlooked and talked about in all my life. I just wanted to run and hide from the entire world at that point. I just didn't understand or realize that the hatred was not because of who I was but rather whose I was.

Oftentimes while I was in the midst of trouble and trials, I couldn't explain it, but it was there that I felt a true sense of familiar peace in God. It was a peace that surpassed even my greatest understanding. Deep down I kept feeling a sense of hope and the ability to continue to move forward no matter what. What I couldn't seem to realize is how it was that one can truly exist and be a part of such a tremendous world with countless of other human beings around them and yet be so alone at the same time.

How could a human being simply go unnoticed in broad daylight? I found that while there were a number of people I could always bare my heart and soul to; it was not always the wisest concept or voice of reasoning. I had to learn that lesson the hard way. Let me tell you, it wasn't one that I would ever want to repeat again...

Even as this book is being written, I recall some family members and friends that have hurt me to the core. And whether they did it intentionally or not, I had to learn that it was not only necessary to move forward, it was imperative that I made a decision to forgive over time and simply kept it moving. That required a lot of dying to self and relinquishing it all over to the Lord. Many nights I cried myself to sleep, asking God why was this happening to me, and why was the pain so excruciating? Often he would say, "No cross, no crown."

However, the more I appeared to be blessed, the more others wanted to attack and hinder the flow of what I believed God had called and fashioned me to be. Some latched on, lied on, and even wished upon me many hurtful things. In the midst of that, they would even smile in my face all the while; sometimes the dagger in their hands had not even cooled off before they were asking for a favor, handout, or leg up...but God!

The more I reacted in a kind, gentle, and humbled spirit the worst some of their treatment or feedback from them I received. For some, the question was, "How did she get that?" For others, it was more of a matter of fact: "She doesn't deserve that." Sadly this became the motto both in and out of church. Still the strangest thing happened during one of my many trials I noticed that God always sent people whom I would least expect to be a comforting support, motivator, activist, and gentle soul into my life.

Often these were people who had no previous history with me, no ties to my well-being or any dealings with my past. They were there to invest in my progress and showed sincere, godly interest, and in some ways, carried me when I felt that I could not go on.

They did not ask anything personally of me. They didn't take from me physically, spiritually, or mentally. They met me right where I was, and they came bearing gifts of various healing balms. The gift of listening and not judging, the gift of protection and not exposure, the gift of friendship and not cut throat and selling me out at the drop of a hat—in other words, they meant it for my good. Sounds like angels in disguise to me. Hebrews 13:2 says, *"Be not forgetful to entertain strangers; for thereby some have entertained angels unawares."*

A BREAKTHROUGH AT LAST

While living in Michigan, I got my very first break at a real job opportunity working for Blue Cross and Blue Shield of Michigan. When I interviewed for the position it was in the dead of winter and what appeared to be one of the coldest days ever. Thank You Jesus, God intervened and allowed me to make it to the interview safely and on time.

One week before the interview, I had already planned a trip to go home to Mississippi. However, after the chance to interview came about, I wasn't going to allow anything or anyone to stop me from what I perceived to be my golden opportunity for change. So I prayed and asked God to open every conceivable door for me, and He did by allowing the interview to be at the right timing. Taking the bus in that winter storm would prove to be nothing short of a miracle that I made it alive to the interview. I was determined to make it happen, and God provided the strength, avenue, and means for me to make it so.

By the actual day of the interview, there was so much snow on the ground, the weatherman advised everyone to simply remain indoors and keep warm. I did not hear those words at all. All I knew was that I had to make it to that interview—it was my one hope to true independence.

So I decided to throw caution to the wind. I prayed, got layered up with at least three sets of clothing, and headed out on the journey to make it to my interview. On the way there, the buses were running what appeared to be every two hours, and even then, one could barely see the buses in sight until they were right up on them.

The snow was so deep it reached up to my thighs. There was no walking fast. Patience that day was definitely my greatest virtue, but I didn't mind because I was going to reach my goal, which meant I was going to get the job. I had already declared and decreed it to be so. I knew in my heart of hearts that God was definitely on my side.

After leaving home at 8:00 a.m., I arrived at my destination around 11:00 a.m. When I made it to the downtown area, I was frozen despite three layers of clothing. I quickly walked a couple of blocks to the building in knee deep snow, changed clothes in the bathroom, and then proceeded upstairs for my interview.

Upon arrival, I was met by a very attractive, slender, smart-looking woman who introduced herself as Ms. Edna Broadus. Everything about her perception shouted confidence, intelligence, and professionalism. I knew then and there that Blue Cross and Blue Shield was the company for me. So I put a smile on my face, reached out my frozen hand, and said, "Hello, my name is Brenda, and I am here for my interview."

Mrs. Broadus appeared very shocked but pleasantly pleased that anyone would go through such trouble to keep their interview time with her, when all the other candidates had already called and cancelled. She asked me, "Why didn't you simply call and reschedule your interview today?"

I said, "Because I needed a job, and cancelling wasn't an option for me. Nothing shorter than death was going to hold me back from moving forward." Mrs. Broadus simply smiled and welcomed me into her office.

The interview went well, and afterward, I made the long, dreadful trek back home. It was agonizing and cold. By the time I made it home, I was extremely thankful and thanking God all the way. My poor feet were frozen solid. After the next couple of days, me and my family left Michigan and travelled to Mississippi.

While I was happy to be home to be honest, I didn't feel that I actually belonged in either location. I wrestled in my spirit about whether to stay or return to the place that was becoming an even greater challenge for me on so many different levels.

While there, my mother and I had an opportunity to talk about things that concerned me a lot. I have always felt really close to my mom, I felt that it would be easy to share almost everything with her. At the same time, I didn't want to burden her with my personal problems or cause her to worry about me being away from home. So I hid a lot of my pain and hurts from her.

Somehow I knew God would work them out in his own timing. I only prayed for Him to provide me with the strength and wisdom I needed to stay in His care and focus. At the end of our conversation, I asked my mother to just pray for me and she said, "Baby, I am."

Often during the conversation, I continuously pretended that everything was okay, when deep down, I never felt so alone, saddened, and hurt in my entire life. I knew that no one in my family would really understand my pain and anguish and probably wouldn't believe me even if I tried to share it. So I made it up in my mind that I would never bother to really talk about it with anyone in particular. Besides, to me, everyone had their own issues and problems to deal with without taking on mine.

On the way back to Michigan, I cried softly and prayed a lot in the car and asked God to please open the necessary doors for me to move forward. I just needed a serious break and only He could provide that outlet for me. On Monday morning, I decided to give Mrs. Broadus a call and remind her of who I was; however, in the process of me attempting to remind Mrs. Broadus of our interview, I was abruptly cut off when Mrs. Broadus suddenly said, "Oh course, I remember who you are. In fact, I made a decision that day to hire you when you left the interview. I was going to give you a call later this week. When can you start?"

To which my reply was, "Was yesterday too early?" We both laughed. After hanging up the phone, I remembered lying on the floor and crying out to God, saying thank you over and over until I was out of breath. I was so very happy for once, a big break had come, and something was finally turning around in my favor. I vowed that very day that I would work hard, do a great job, and show God just how grateful I really was to have this amazing opportunity for myself.

From day one, I absolutely loved my new assignment and could not wait to start my new independence of coming into my own. Daily when arriving to work, I poured my all into my new workload. My boss often praised me and we became instant friends who would often go shopping together after work. After several years of working for Mrs. Broadus, I was promoted to various other positions within the company. Eventually, I was offered the role of supervisor over the claims department. I eagerly accepted that role.

After several years of working at Blue Cross Blue Shield, I was able to rent my first home, and even purchase my first car, all on my own. I was very excited about moving forward. After a while, I started attending college and began taking courses as a Court Reporter. I wondered if I should change my major or continue in the role I had already began. Nevertheless, I continued to grow successfully but not without challenges.

AN UNUSUAL ENCOUNTER

By now, I had met this wonderful guy while attending Detroit Court Reporting College. I was enrolled in their court reporting program where I had worked my way up to a senior-level court reporter, which meant my shorthand speed was averaging 180 words per minute. (The goal was 225.)

This young man name was Audie Murphy. While I thought he was funny, attractive, and attentive, he didn't at first appeal to be my personal type. In fact, the last thing that I was looking for at that time was a boyfriend. I was much too serious about building a career and making a life for myself and that did not seriously include a boyfriend or a significant other.

Audie was persistent nonetheless. One day while Audie and I were between classes, he decided to come over to my locker. He introduced himself to me and asked me very candidly if he could share my locker with me for a couple of days. Stunned by the sheer request, I asked him, "Excuse me, are you talking to me?" And his reply was, "Ah, yes." Honestly, I thought not only is he rude, but he is not currently operating off a full tank, and I didn't have time for this. So once again, I said, "Ah, no, you cannot, and besides, why don't you ask your buddies that you are hanging out with?"

He was relentless in his approach and kept making excuse after excuse as to why he could not ask them and that it would only be for a couple of days until he was assigned to his own locker. Late for class, I reluctantly agreed against my better judgment, wisdom, and obviously common sense.

Needless to say, I never got my key back from him, nor was my "personal" locker ever the same. Jesus, take the wheel! I didn't want to go to prison over what I deemed to be my personal and private space, but the child was just plain arrogant and clueless.

After months of realizing that I was never going to get my key back from Audie, I began plotting ways of getting rid of him from my life and my personal locker by any means necessary! By now, he has started asking me out to the movies, to the park, parties, and he even asked me can he come over to see me from time to time? Okay, I would have to admit that what I really liked about Audie was his zest for life and his obvious confidence he had about himself.

He was outgoing, confident, sweet, attentive, compassionate, and conceited all at the same time. To me, he was also a little self-assured when he wanted to be which got on my last African American nerve. One day we agreed to go on a date to the movies and so we exchanged our telephone numbers, and I finally decided to give him a call to make sure that we were still on.

His brother answered the phone and when he went to get him and Audie answered the phone, I said, "Hello, how are you?" To my surprise, he said, "Hello, Debra, how are you?" "Debra? Are you serious?" I then hung up the phone and didn't speak to him for at least a week. He pleaded and said that he was so sorry at least twenty different times. I was furious, which only made matters worse.

Then one day as I was walking to the bus stop after class with a classmate, whose name is Debra, she asked me, in a giggly voice, "Brenda, is that boy trying to talk to you?" I asked, "Who?" She said, "I think his name is Audie. He was trying to talk to me and gave me his phone number. When I said that I have a boyfriend, he said that doesn't matter."

Well, let me tell you that only added potential fuel to the makeshift fire. When Audie called me again, I inquired about Debra, and he said, "Oh, I remember asking some girl for her phone number, but it wasn't any big deal." Men! Over time, Audie and I continued to talk more and more. All of a sudden, I noticed that my male friends, who used to eagerly ask me out to lunch and offer me a ride home, began fading away mysteriously. I noticed weeks had gone by before this type of generosity took place between me and some of my male friends.

Curious, I began to pay more attention to things around me. One day I approached one of my male friends who was upset with me and said that Audie had approached them and said, "Hey, why are you asking my girlfriend out to lunch behind my back? You need to back off."

To my surprise, not only was I dumbfounded, but I was also angry and embarrassed by this. Audie and I were not boyfriend and girlfriend by any means. So when I saw him later that day in the hallway, I asked him point-blank, "Did you tell my friends that we were dating?" And he said, with a grin, "I sure did because we are in my mind." Precious Lord, take my hand…

As time passed by, Audie and I continued to hang out as what I thought of as friends, but more and more Audie continued to say that we were dating and refused to see it any other way. Well, by now, privately, although originally, Audie was not what I would have considered as my "type." He was beginning to grow on me, although Lord knows I tried every trick in the book to get rid of him.

I remember one particular time that stuck out in my mind specifically as it relates to "us dating." I was plotting to make it known to Audie that we were not dating, so I typed a letter to myself from this mystery guy named "Charles," who really did exist in my class. In fact, he was an accounting major and very smart, handsome, and older than me. However, Charles never gave me the time of day. So I decided to use his name because in my opinion, it would not appear to be obvious that I wrote the letter to myself.

I set a date and put the plot into action. After I wrote this very romantic and funny letter, I carefully accepted an invitation out to the movies with Audie for that next weekend but invited him over earlier in the week so that we could study together. (Man, I'll show him! At least that's what I thought.) Well, the night was going just the way I had originally planned it.

Like clockwork, the doorbell ranged right on cue and Mr. Murphy entered, looking all GQ'ed walking in with his Michigan swagger and acting like he was the very best thing God had ever made. Ha, little did he know I had something special for him. I greeted him with a Southern girl smile. "Hello," and invited him in and deliberately left my typed "love letter" on the coffee table, sticking slightly out of my work-book so it would grab his attention as I took my time preparing the snacks.

The moral to the plot was that he would read the letter, get upset, and leave; thus, the relationship/friendship would then be officially over, and maybe I could have my personal life back. Well, apparently I underestimated Mr. Murphy, and the joke ended up being on me. For starters, unbeknownst to me, he had read the letter five minutes after I had left the room, placed it back into the same book. He wasn't moved in the least by my failed setup attempt to imply my letter was from another man.

Audie appeared to be unimpressed and unnerved by the entire thing. Not only was he not moved by the letter, but he made no attempt to help me pick up the pieces of the letter scattered all over the floor. He didn't ask me what was wrong or what was going on or anything. He just continued to pretend that he was studying and engaged in his homework. And here I was apologizing for this mishap when all of a sudden he turns to me and said, "Brenda, I know that you typed that letter to yourself. Give it a rest."

Embarrassed, tickled, and about to burst at the seams with laughter from my personal embarrassment, I still pretended like I didn't know what he was alluding to. In the midst of it all, I had the nerve to say, "Oh my god, are you really accusing me of being so desperate that I would actually take the time to type a letter to myself and try to fool someone with it?" Audie looked at me without blinking an eye and said, "Yes! Now are we going to get down to studying or are you through pretending?" I looked at him, and all I could think of at that moment was how I would look in an orange jump suit and how many years it would cost me to pay it off.

He continued his little antics by saying, "Because no man in his right mind writes a letter to a woman using so many flowery words. A real man just gets straight to the point." I thought this man is crazier than I originally recognized. He absolutely must go. Let the plotting continue…

By the time our study night was over, I never experienced so much egg on my face in my entire life. It became crystal clear that this one was not going to be easy to get rid of. I must do my due diligence in making sure that my next plot sticks.

God help me, but as time went by, I really began to enjoy Audie's company more and more, and I actually looked forward to spending time with him. The problem was he had this very outgoing personality, warmth, and certain charisma about himself that made him extremely popular with the ladies—and that's the last thing I wanted and/or needed. So I figured it would be better to go our separate ways rather than get too close to someone who would not be true to one person.

Over time, Audie became my best friend, someone I could really trust and confide in. I found him to be reliable, dependable, and a very good listener. We shared a lot of good times as well as personal goals, dreams, and visions that we desired for ourselves in the future. In Audie's family, there were four brothers and one sister. Audie is the baby of his family, go figure! When I was introduced to his father, I immediately fell in love with Mr. Murphy. To me, Mr. Murphy, known by his family as "Pops" was the epitome of what a good father was supposed to be. He was strong, caring, funny, gentle, and supportive. He loved his family, and cooking for them was one of the major ways he expressed his love to them.

Mr. Murphy had an outgoing spirit and personality as well. He also had a quick wit about himself that everyone close to him waited on whenever they were fortunate to be in his company. Whenever I was around him, I always felt welcomed and an important part of their family. Mr. Murphy loved to cook Creole food and pretended that he was from Louisiana. He could be found many days wearing his white chef hat and jacket. When he was in the kitchen, he was always talking as if he were actually from New Orleans or someplace along those lines. He made me laugh often until tears rolled down my face.

One thing about it, I quickly realized that the more I got to know Mr. Murphy, whether my relationship with his son went any further or not, we would always remain friends because of the easiness of our ability to relate to each other. In time, Mr. Murphy made me feel special and a vital part of his family.

After dating for approximately two years, I finally shared with Audie quite a bit of personal history about myself—and why I didn't trust easily or allow anyone to get too close to me without pushing them away. Fearing that he too would walk away, I decided it was the best thing to do and that the timing was right in knowing what future place I could actually hold in his life; if he was unwilling to be a part of my life for the long haul, he needed to leave now and not look back with no regrets.

After talking and sharing my heart with Audie, not only did my sharing bring the two of us closer together, it also allowed me to see his heart and the fact that I could rest in Audie's love for me. The sincerity Audie provided to me made me feel comfortable in believing that I could rely upon him no matter what. As

Audie and I continued to share in conversation, he told me about the passing of his mother during his last year of high school and how painful that was for him to accept at such a young age.

He acknowledged the severity of his loss and how he was angry with God at first for taking her from his young life. In a lot of ways, he felt very guilty and ashamed for not spending more time with her on the many occasions she had asked him to. His response would be, "Mom, I have basketball practice, or I am going to meet the guys for football practice. I'll be home soon and then we can talk." He said his mother would always smile and just say, "Okay, son. You go ahead." Sadly Audie didn't know that he would not have as much time as he thought he would with this mother.

What a horrible thing to happen at any age, but especially during high school when one is just trying to make sense of it all. The news of his mother's passing was devastating to him and rightfully so. For a while, he became distant and withdrawn.

He would tell me later that losing his mother was the worst pain any human being could endure.

To Audie, the death of his mother, in some ways, brought him and his dad much closer and strengthened them both in other ways. Over time, they became distant again. While his father was dealing with the loss of the love of his wife, the mother of his children, and perhaps his best friend, Audie was trying to learn new ways with how to cope with the loss of his mother and bridging the gap in communication between him and his dad. Over the years, things worked themselves out, and they became closer than ever.

They absolutely adored each other, and whenever Mr. Murphy spoke of him in conversation, one could readily see the love and joy he had for Audie on his face and in his voice, Audie also echoed the same sentiments towards him. I was happy to see two well-deserved people recognized that they truly needed and dearly loved each other.

A NEW CHAPTER BEGINS

After dating for more than two years, Audie asked me to go for a visit over to his dad's house. He needed to pick up some records and albums he was planning to use at a house party later that week. Reluctantly I agreed, and we went over to visit his dad. The problem was Audie lied to me, but in a good way. It was a nice evening. The snow was coming down lightly, and his dad had a nice fire going. Audie asked me to stay upstairs with his father, while he went into the basement to look for the music he was going to be using.

Sensing the atmosphere was a little different; I became very nervous about the evening and hoped that Audie would hurry up and come back upstairs and rejoin the conversation, which wasn't much because all I could think to talk about, believe it or not, was the weather report. I was so extremely nervous, and I kept repeating myself. "I think it is supposed to snow all night tonight." "Did you hear that it is supposed to become very, very cold over the weekend?"

All alone, I kept thinking, what is wrong with you? Change the subject for goodness' sake. I felt like I was on this emotional rollercoaster and that I absolutely could not get off of it to save my life!

By the time Audie did rejoin the family, I was very uncomfortable because not only was I struggling to maintain a decent conversation with Audie's dad, now three brothers had in fact showed up to join the conversation. Dear God, help me, I exclaimed; I was sweating, nervous, and praying, "Jesus, take the wheel, please."

After Audie resurfaced, he chit-chatted for a few minutes and then got down on one knee and asked me to marry him right then and there in front of his brothers—Rodney, Emmitt, and Michael—as well as Mr. Murphy. I thought that I would drop right then and there. Excited, nervous, surprised, and extremely happy, I said yes!

I shared the news with my own family and friends later. While the majority of my family celebrated the moment with me, there were a few who suggested that I was too young and perhaps throwing my "whole" life away too soon. What none of them knew or realized was that at the age of nineteen, I didn't even have a boyfriend, let alone entertained the thought of being engaged or being married early.

I prayed and asked God when He was ready, and if marriage indeed was a part of His will for my life, to please make my husband up from scratch. I asked God not to give me a man too young that mentally he would respond as my son and don't give me someone too old that it would be like being married to my father. But to please give me some one who would be absolutely just right for me.

During our engagement, Audie and I couldn't quite settle down on an appropriate wedding day and changed our minds several times. Finally we agreed to wait until the timing was just right for us. However, one day in 1984, after arriving home from work, I received a call from my future father-in-law, who I lovingly referred to as Pops. At first, he sounded his usual self, full of joy in his voice, nothing too serious; but later during our phone conversation, everything changed radically.

His nickname for me was Kid. He said, "Heah, Kid, I've got something very important that I need to tell you, and it is important that you pay close attention to me." Even though it scared me to listen, I took a deep breath and asked what was it? Mr.

Murphy continued, saying, "I have had a lot of health issues lately and have been seeing my doctor regularly. The doctor is telling me that I only have approximately one month to live due to my heart condition, and because I am refusing to have open heart surgery, this is it. I do not want you to share this information with anyone else, especially Peewee."

Not only was I not ready for this type of news, I didn't want to hear it, and I told him so. I was crying hysterically, and he asked me to please stop so that I could hear what he had to say. He trusted me and he wanted me to know that everything was going to be okay. He continued by saying, "I love you and I love the way you and my son interact together. He's a good man and will make you a good husband someday. I want you to please promise me that you and he will stick together and that you will always take good care of him no matter what, okay? I taught him well, and I know that he is a good man."

After receiving a call that Mr. Murphy had had a massive heart attack at home and was being taken to the hospital via EMS, Audie and I headed out to meet the rest of the family there. Not only was this a difficult time for the immediate family members, but there was also a terrible storm brewing that night.

My heart ached in trying to prepare Audie for the news of his dad. With every word, tears streamed down my face. All I wanted to do was hold him close and console him. In that moment, I wasn't really sure if my tears were just for Audie or the both of us because I loved Mr. Murphy dearly as well.

Looking back on earlier that same day, I realized that I had driven by Mr. Murphy's house and stopped but didn't see his car and assumed that he wasn't home. Later, when he called to say that he was home but didn't reach the door in time and saw me when I was leaving. I was so sorry that I missed him because I really and truly enjoyed his company.

The news took my breath away, and for a minute even though I was trying to be strong for Audie, I was struggling to keep my head up above water myself. Audie and I just held on to each other as tightly as we could and prayed for strength to endure the difficult task before us.

The next several days were just a blur. The both of us could barely function at work. When I went to work the next day, I was crying so much that my boss called me in and asked me what was wrong. I told her that my father had passed. My boss sent me home. Later that night, I felt so badly about telling my boss a lie that I could not find any peace and I decided to tell her the next day that it wasn't my father but my fiancé's father, who was just like a real dad to me. She thanked me for telling her the truth so that I would not get into any trouble for fabricating a lie. She also sent me some beautiful red roses in memory of him as well.

By the time we reached the appropriate hospital and actually found where Pops was taken, it was raining really badly. Audie was driving. He just parked the car and got out in the rain and walked into the hospital. When I got myself together, I got out and came in to look for Audie, thinking that Pops was okay. I eventually met an officer who asked how he could help me. I told the officer that I was looking for the Murphy family. He instructed me to continue down the hall and make a left turn the room would be on the left.

However, the room that I should have gone into was on the right where the family had gathered together. Unfortunately I took the direction of the officer and when I entered the room, it was where Mr. Murphy's body laid. I screamed and called out his name, "Pops, no, no, no." No one came, and I was assumed no one even heard me screaming and calling his name. I was so very overwhelmed and kept saying, "Mr. Murphy, Mr. Murphy please wake up, and please don't leave us now. Not now, not ever, we so need you." I held him in my arms.

He was still warm and appeared as though he was only sleeping I swore he had a slight smile on his face. I grieved him badly. I missed him already; his voice, his smile, his sense of humor, and his wisdom. At that very moment, I felt like I had just lost my dearest friend in the entire world. I couldn't stand, I couldn't breathe, my legs felt like lead. Nothing at that particular moment made any sense. I just kept wondering, No God, not now. We need him so much. Please, God, not now, Mr. Murphy, please do not leave us. We need you.

My heart ached for the family, especially Audie. Here he was only twenty-one years of age, and he had already lost his mother and now his father. I feared for him, how he was going to move forward and what if anything could I do to help him. Thankfully, I knew how to pray and get my prayers answered

By the end of the week, funeral plans had been made, and everything was set in motion for Pops funeral. Audie and I primarily made all the arrangements. It was difficult at best. However, everyone in the end pulled together for the most part and made it a wonderful ceremony.

Shortly after the funeral, Audie was really suffering a lot from the loss but handled it like a true trooper. For the first time, I really saw the man I knew he was becoming in full bloom. By August of that same year, Audie visited the Air Force recruiting department and decided whether his future would belong in the military or to remain in Michigan where he had just been offered a new position.

After all, his dad had once served in the Navy, and Audie wanted to follow in his dad's footsteps. By that next year, he had actually enlisted and was off to the United States Air Force by August 1985. I threw him a going-away party. No one knew he had enlisted but me, who actually encouraged him to go because he needed that time alone to grow and become all that he deserved to be.

Audie had too much potential to become anything less than the man God had called and designed him, and I would be anything less than a potential wife, friend, and confidante to stand by him and watch him do anything less.

"Not on my watch," I would say. Knowing that Audie had experienced a lot of pain and sorrow at such a tender age in his life, I gave him a going-away party because he would be leaving soon to join the United States Air Force. The party for Audie was bittersweet and I knew that I would miss him terribly.

I questioned myself whether I had done the right thing by encouraging Audie to go. That night after the party, Audie asked me to tell him if I had changed my mind about him leaving, and if so, he wouldn't go. I knew in my heart of heart, without a shadow of a doubt, it was the right thing for him to do. In the end, it was still Audie's final decision to make, and I was very proud of him for taking the stand no matter what or who didn't like it.

The days and weeks afterward were very challenging and difficult. I missed him very much and thought of him often. I could not keep in touch as much because this was during Audie's basic training timeframe and he wasn't allowed to communicate with anyone outside of the training camp yet because he needed to stay focused. So I prayed for him daily, that his strength would not fail him.

Within three weeks, I finally received my first letter from Audie and boy had he changed already. The first letter that I got I could hardly believe that it was actually from him because it sounded so mature. It was written with so much conviction and assurance. All of a sudden it seemed that he was certain about a lot of things and choices that he had made in particular and he said so. I wrote back to him often and kept telling him how much I loved him and how proud I was of the man he was developing daily into.

WHAT A DIFFERENCE A DAY MAKES

One month after Audie left Michigan, I was robbed at gunpoint in broad daylight right outside of a convenience store with onlookers standing right next to me. I remembered there was a man to my left standing close to my car, having a full-fledged conversation with a female while I was being robbed and said and did nothing. He didn't care or even looked concerned.

While I was being robbed, I prayed and asked God for his divine protection. I just kept repeating, "God, please don't let me die this way or out in a field some place all alone. Protect me and see me through." During this time, the ring leader with the gun ordered me to give him all of my jewelry, my purse, and to get in the car and drive away.

He told me, "Look, b____, I will absolutely blow your mother-f—— brains out and never look back. If necessary, I will kill your mother, father and your f——g family. I don't care about you or anybody else. Now get in your car now!"

I was so angry and standing in total disbelief and shock, I quickly jumped into my car and followed the robbers to a house they entered into nearby. On the way there, I observed them walking down the streets laughing and unzipping my purse, taking out my personal things one by one. My cash, sunglasses, and other items that was important to me. I watched them go up to this particular house where I wrote down the address and sped off to the nearest police station to report what just happened.

To my horror, I found out the police was in no hurry to take the police report or to assist me. To me that was completely unacceptable, but after all, what could I do about it, if the police didn't care, I knew most likely no one else outside of them who cared about me would as well.

After leaving the police department I realized that I missed Audie tremendously. Although I longed to talk with him regarding the issue, I did not want to alarm him and cause him to worry about me. After the robbery, I immediately called my brother Jake and told him what happened to me. My brother replied, "Faye, I hate to tell you this, but you were targeted and setup by the guy standing next to your car who probably suspected that you were not from that particular neighborhood and tipped off the other guys, and that's how the robbery went off without a hitch."

Hearing my brother say those words caused tears to roll down my face in anguish. I was frightened and extremely angry with the fact that those thugs had temporarily stolen everything that I had worked so hard to thrive in; my peace, confidence, and temporarily my joy, not to mention the obvious, keys to my home, credit cards, wallet, and identification cards.

I thought the one place I called sacred, my home, has now been marked as a potential target for outsiders to now invade at their leisure. I no longer felt protected or secured. For months after the robbery, I felt scared, nervous, and afraid to go out of my home for fear of what or who I might find lurking outside waiting for me or for that matter, what I might find upon my return back home.

When Audie's brother Emmitt told him about the incident, he was hurt and angry and wished he could have been there to protect me. The truth of the matter, I really wished the same, but I knew deep down inside that God had me in that hour and that Audie needed to remain focused.

I continued to pray and really seek God about what to do because I didn't want this incident to totally cause me to never trust another living being ever again in my life. I had truly come a long ways in that regard. Even though I walked, worked, and interacted with various individuals on a daily basis, I never quite felt really safe, and I always wondered and questioned just about everyone that I personally came into contact with.

Finally, one day, I shared with a coworker about my misfortune, and to my surprise, she began telling me about a watch she had bought from some guys that sold it to her for a "hot" price. What? So I asked her to show me the watch, and when she did, the first thing that I did was look on the back of it.

Low and behold, it was my watch! My initials and birthday were inscribed on it, as I had requested it when I bought it. When I asked her how much she paid for the watch, she said she only paid fifty dollars for it. My heart sunk, and then my blood began to boil because that was a very expensive watch, to which I had paid five hundred dollars.

When the woman recognized my facial expression concerning the watch, she asked me if there was something wrong, I wanted to say, "Ah, yeah, you just bought my stolen watch and only paid fifty dollars whereas I had worked very hard and purchased it the right way." Nevertheless, I offered to give her $75.00 for the watch, and she immediately took the watch back and put it in her purse and changed the subject. Well as you probably guessed it by now, I never saw my watch again not that day or ever.

As I previously mentioned, after that incident, my trust became heavily guarded and possibly overly protected. If someone walked too close to me, I immediately became offensive and defensive. If someone I didn't know asked me questions about anything, directions, or just general conversation, I would ignore them or simply shrug my shoulders and say, "I don't know."

I was slowly becoming very disconnected from people in general, and I wanted it that way. I couldn't get over the mentality of a thug and how they operate. In that moment, all I had for that mentality of a people were sheer hate, hostility, and absolutely zero tolerance for their actions.

I didn't care if they lived in a certain neighborhood, didn't have a home at all, or simply slept under a tree in the middle of the streets. It gives no one the right to steal and threaten another human being's life for what is rightfully and lawfully theirs, and the mere thought that the police responded even the more to a citizen who just needed assistance in such an unprofessional and infantile manner even further solidified the fact that I was in the wrong city, wrong side of town, wrong state, and apparently dealing with the wrong people. I wanted out as far away from human beings with this kind of mentality as humanly possible.

Thankfully time went by quickly. In September 1985, Audie called me and said, "Babe, I have a date in mind that we should get married if you still want to marry me, let's do this. By then, I was more than ready to do so and could not wait for him to say it. He suggested November 23, 1985. I hurriedly agreed and began working on the plans immediately. I was so thankful and excited about getting married, moving away, and starting over in a brand new city with my honey! I could hardly stand it.

On Saturday, November 23, 1985, I married the absolute love of my life. We were beaming from ear to ear. My sister Vera was the matron of honor. My bridesmaids were Sharon, Betty, Lisa, and Kimberly. My flower girl was none other than Ms. Shanita Scott, who threw very few flower petals as I recall—it doesn't matter—she looked quite cute while doing so.

The groomsmen were Al, Wayne, Larry, and Emmitt. Willie was Audie's best man. My beloved big brother Jake, Jr. walked me down the aisle that day. It was incredible, and he complimented me on my dress and wished me the best. I believed that he was proud of me…

I must say, it meant the world to me to have my big brother say those words to me. On that day, there were lots of people in attendance who meant a lot to both Audie and me. There was my mother, Frances; my sister Pearlie, who had travelled from Mississippi to be with us; Dorothy and Laura, who already lived in Detroit; and one of my closest nieces Sherry, who also came from Mississippi and was a part of the wedding. There were also a host of special cousins from Chicago—Ruth, Bonnie, Mary, and Annette—and other locations. To me, that was one of the happiest days of my life.

THE DAY AFTER THE WEDDING

After tying the knot, I must have cried for the next twenty-four hours, wondering what exactly had I gotten myself into. It was never a question of whether I loved Audie or wanted to spend the rest of my life with him. It was, literally, what had I done.

Was I truly ready for this gigantic step? What I loved about my relationship with God was that he instantly brought me back to a personal conversation that I had had with him when I was nineteen years of age and was not even in search of a boyfriend, let alone than a husband.

I remembered asking God to make me a husband up from scratch because I only wanted to do this once. When I heard God's voice remind me of our previous conversation, I was immediately reassured that I had indeed done the right thing and that I could be at peace with it all.

Audie and I celebrated our very first Thanksgiving together in Michigan. The following Friday after Thanksgiving, Audie had to leave on Saturday to return to Fort Worth, Texas to report to his new duty station. Originally, Audie and I agreed to him coming back for me in March. Once he got settled into his first active duty role, he looked for an apartment for the two of us. That was fine with me because I still had my job at Blue Cross Blue Shield in downtown Detroit.

I told my family that I would probably be moving around March 1986 once Audie got everything settled in Fort Worth for us. Well, things didn't quite work out that way for us. Turns out, when Audie returned back to Fort Worth, he was told by his officer that he didn't really need to be back until Tuesday after Thanksgiving. That didn't go over to well with him and to tell you the truth, with me either; any who, time marched on, and before we knew it, Audie called me one night in January and said, "Heah, babe. I am coming to get you within the next couple of weeks." I said, "Oh, really? Are you serious?"

He said, with total clarity, "Um hum. Yes, I am, and I need for you to be ready." Of course, I was excited, nervous, a little scared, and did not want to share the news with anyone else let alone my job because I sort of promised my boss that I would not leave until March, oh boy!

For the next several weeks, I told no one my news. I hoped and prayed that when I did, everyone would be happy for me and totally understand. To begin with, my boss said immediately to me, "Wait a minute you promised me that you would stay until March. What am I supposed to do with you leaving? Give me a few days to think this over. Are you sure this cannot be worked out, I mean it's almost March, give or take a month or two." She laughed. Then she offered me more money, a promotion, additional time off to go "visit" with Audie and everything. I could literally hear my heart beating within my chest cavity walls and that was the easy side of things.

Wait until my family finds out, I thought to myself; one by one, I began to tell my family, and for the most part, I believed they all took it pretty well; however, it is always the unspoken word that no one really says that is heard the loudest.

Well, the second week of January 1986 rolled around, and Audie flew home like he said he would and rented a truck for our move. He could not have come in a worse time. The snow was so high you could barely see the porch of our house. To say it was cold was a severe understatement. As Audie and I began to pack, we began to reminisce about what we would miss most about life in Michigan and what we actually would not.

We talked mostly about the house parties that we would throw on the weekends with our families, or the weekend Calvary's that we couldn't wait to get to on Friday/Saturday nights to get our dance on out on the dance floor. Yep, we thought, those were the good old days.

For me an Audie, it was difficult saying goodbye to our families. Leaving was indeed bittersweet. Looking back on it all, it was necessary to do so because we were starting our lives together and needed to be with each other. To make sure it would be a success would mean we needed to move forward.

Audie and I traveled from Michigan to Memphis, and we were immediately sought after by a trucker on the expressway that was apparently headed to Memphis, Tennessee as well. He noticed that the chain pulling our vehicle was loose and that we needed to immediately fix it.

The trucker did everything noticeably to make Audie and me aware of this problem including drastically cutting us off the expressway and letting us know that we were in danger of losing our car and possibly having a serious accident. We thanked the trucker profusely, and he assisted us with getting the car-and-chain matter situated properly and got back on the road. The trucker advised us to follow him to Memphis since that was his usual route weekly. Man following him was one of the best adventures we ever had. This was the beginning of many adventures to come.

True enough, Audie and I reached Memphis by six that evening. Thereafter we checked into our hotel room grabbed something to eat and planned our route for the next day's adventure. Early that next morning, we got up and got dressed, checked the truck out and got on the road again. Next stop was Fort Worth, Texas.

As we approached Dallas, Texas that evening, we came across this very hilly section just when the sun was going down. Boy, oh boy, was that not a wonderful sight to behold! We both were in awe of God's beauty. Whoa, hello, Texas! We're here!

THE BIG MOVE...ON MY OWN

"For I know the plans I have for you,"
declares the Lord, "plans to prosper you and not to harm
you, plans to give you hope and a future."

—Jeremiah 29:11

By 9:30 p.m., Audie and I made it to Fort Worth. He stopped and grabbed the keys to our new humble abode. As we entered the apartments, we could smell the newness of our first apartment together. Audie had taken care of everything. In fact, he had taken the rest of the week off and had requested that some of his friends come over and help us get everything into the apartment.

One of the first things I noticed immediately about Texas was the heat. Man, what a complete difference it was between Michigan and Texas. In Michigan it seems to be below zero in the winter whereas in Texas it was always above a hundred it seems, and here I was travelling with all winter clothes—boots with fur in them, sweaters, hoodies, sweatshirts, and corduroys.

Boy what an eye-opener I received. The next several weeks and months were spent unpacking, setting up the apartment, and looking for employment. Although Audie encouraged me not to rush into it, I knew that it was the next best thing for me to do—either find reputable employment or look into completing my court reporting degree. After searching for a while, eventually I selected a school called Arlington Court Reporting College. I finished my remaining courses!

I graduated valedictorian and gave the graduating speech. Afterward, my instructor asked me who wrote it for me; I remarked I did. The instructor asked me for a copy. I gave her the original and moved forward.

Life was exciting for the next couple of months. I got to work in the legal office at Carswell Air Force Base under the leadership of Judge Colonel Michael J. Fox during depositions real time. One day, while working on base, a plane actually crashed into the lake directly behind the base; it shut everything down for hours.

No traffic was to move on or off the base itself. Because I was already on the base and in the courtroom, I had no choice but to continue writing and covering the live story as it unfolded. I was asked to stay and continue the processing of the deposition until the matter was completed. Of course I said yes! It was one of the most exciting times of my court reporting career.

I was offered the job as full-time court reporter for Carswell Air Force Base, and the paperwork was in motion. However, when the other individual who was already employed there realized that I was interested in the role as well, he because upset and setup road blocks to keep it from materializing. Needless to say, I was never offered the job. I was disappointed but not distraught to where I could not and did not move forward.

I decided it was best to move on and to enjoy the moment that I had there. From that point, I was offered an opportunity to do some internship work under Judge H. in the Tarrant County Courthouse in Fort Worth, Texas.

It was fun, exciting, invigorating, and stimulating. Judge H. was absolutely a no-none sense person and she took no prisoners. I really liked her personality and spirit. She had hutzpah. From that moment in time, I actually taught a court reporting course at a Court Reporting College for over a year. That was great because I had the opportunity to make a tremendous difference in the lives of my students to personally mentor them, challenge them, and pray for them that they would never give up and go on to reach their greatest potential.

Over the course of the next several years, I worked for different law firms as legal secretaries, office managers, receptionist, and etc. Although it was interesting, I would absolutely never want to do it again. That entire environment is too crazy. For me, I have gained expertise in divorce, workers compensation, traffic warrants, and family law. Out of all of my experiences and exposure, I don't know which was worse—the clients or the bosses. I think that the jury is still out on all of them!

There was one legal secretary position that I will never forget while working in Texas. I was hired by a legal firm that happens to operate in the specialty of workers compensation. One of my many roles was to process all of the clients' workers compensation claims, following up with the clients, making any doctor appointments and scheduling any meetings that needed to be made in the office concerning the clients.

This particular client that I was introduced to was about sixty years old and appeared to be sweet, loving, and even kind over the phone. In other words at the moment, the client thought that I represented the best thing since slice bread during that moment in time...um-hum!

Well, bless my sweet heart. One day I had to call and schedule an appointment for her workers' compensation claim. The client agreed to come in and said, "See ya at 1:00 p.m., honey." Upon arrival, the client's dear hubby came in the door first, which opened to my back; and when I turned around, the look on my client's husband's face was as if he had personally seen another episode of Roots up close and personal! The uncut version! He was really trying to discourage his wife from coming in to the office by pushing her out of the door as she was shuffling trying to get in.

Well, between the entire ruckus in the hallway and the phone ringing in my office, she finally got into the building when she saw me sitting there. She literally yelled as loudly as her little old lungs would allow her to. "Oh my god, you are black!"

I only found it benefitting to stand as well and say proudly from behind my desk and yelled, "Oh my god, can someone please get it off of me, what is it? How did it get on me, please help me get it off of me, can someone help me please?"

Not only did it draw attention from the entire office, but I was in total disbelief as to why the client had this surprised look on her face that I was acting this way. In fact, the look on the client's face said, "Don't you know that you are black?" And I guess the look on mine read, "No, I don't realize that I'm black because that's the pigmentation of my skin. There is more to me than my skin color."

I am Brenda, the one you have been telling all your personal business to." Interestingly enough, not one time during the phone conversations did the client ever ask me what skin color I might have been because it didn't matter at the moment, and neither did it matter to me afterwards, it still doesn't matter today.

The performance went on for about two hours between me sobbing off and on. During this entire time, the entire office looked dumbfounded, crazy, bewildered, and just plain confused as to how all of this got out of hand in the first place. Eventually, I went home for the day, stating that I could not work under those stressful conditions. I stayed home for the next two weeks, to which my job paid me for my time off. After that, I never looked back even after they called me several times and asked for me.

PURCHASING OUR FIRST HOUSE

After being in Texas for several months and living in our first apartment together, Audie and I decided that we should look for our first house; I more than Audie was more than ready to move forward with the search.

During choir rehearsal one night I shared with a friend about my desire for purchasing a new home to which the friend replied "Well, let's just pray about it" right then and there we held hands together and did just that, it was a Friday night.

Later during that Friday night into the wee hours of the morning, I felt strongly that God had heard our prayers and what we had touch and agreed upon by the Holy Spirit and how I felt the functioning of the Holy Spirit urging "Get up, I have a house for you." I never looked back or doubted, believe it or not, when I heard that voice, it was with such conviction, that I didn't even look for an excuse not to believe it. I didn't second guess what I heard, and I didn't even wake Audie up. I just jumped up, ran to the bathroom took a shower and got dressed.

After getting dressed, I ran down stairs to the newspaper stand and grabbed a paper. As I was turning the pages, I saw this new development over in the Meadow Creek area. I had no idea how to locate it or the homes located in that particular area, but I moved because I believed I had heard the voice of God compelling me to do so. What I did have was a tank full of gas, a mustard seed of faith, and God as my forerunner—and that was enough for me. When Audie saw that I was serious, about moving forward, he said, "Wait a minute! This is crazy, but I am going with you."

I drove, and Audie read the map. After finding the location, we quickly realized that the area was undeveloped, and there was absolutely nothing over there but cats, dogs, owls, wolves, and other varmints that had no place to call home. As we continued to drive in a daze, I prayed even the more because I could feel Audie's "I told you so" moments coming on any second now.

Thank you, Jesus! My prayers and travailing paid off marvelously. Just when my hope was fading just a tad, lo and behold I looked across this pasture and saw a few houses in the distance with a sign that read G. Homes. After picking out the paint swatches, colors of carpet, tile for the bathroom and counter tops, walk through and redlining, they were finally ready to move in. When Audie found out the closing cost was only $1.00 to move in, he almost fainted.

I got a call at work informing me that we were all ready to go and that we needed to bring one dollar to closing with us. Audie almost fainted with joy. Once the closing was over and we were ready to move into our brand new beautiful home, I got a very urgent feeling in the pit of my stomach to have the house blessed first and foremost.

Audie looked at me as if I had lost my mind. I tried time and time again to explain the importance of it all, but he wasn't having it because it was going to be on a Super Bowl Sunday. Forgetting the fact that God had just entrusted us with our first eighty-thousand dollar home, he wanted to celebrate the Cowboys, whom he would never meet. Go figure!

Well, I stood by what I believed the Holy Spirit was leading me to do because I knew God's voice. Besides, the feeling just simply would not go away. The planning began, and the invitations were sent out for the housewarming. I asked the pastor of our church if he would come and bless the house.

To my surprise, he also looked shocked and puzzled. I knew then that I was in for trouble after that. Not only did I pray but I also threw in fasting because I needed it for good measure!

Through much prayer, fasting, lamenting, and praying some more, the people came and so did pastor. I didn't know who was the saddest—the pastor or Audie because they really wanted to watch the game and not pray over a house and eat politely. I didn't care; the house was going to be blessed even if I had to do it alone.

Still feeling a bit of uneasiness, I continued to pray and seek the face of God for more clarity about why I felt this way. Even though no fiery response came, I felt compelled to continue to pray without ceasing, and I did so. On that Friday night, at the end of the week of the housewarming party, I came home after work, cooked, and ate dinner, cleaned up a bit and then went to bed because I had to work the next day. At the time, I was working for an insurance company, so I said good night to Audie who was up watching the game on the couch.

After we moved in, we only had about three neighbors on the entire block. There were no other houses built. Even though it was a little spooky to be living on a block where for the most part, it was pitch black at night, I still felt relatively safe in my own home. After going to bed around 9:30 p.m., I suddenly woke up in the wee hours of the morning due to sensing a very strong presence of someone standing directly over me. While I sensed that evil presence, I was unable to move as if someone was deliberately holding me down. I wasn't scared because it felt peaceful, but I was directed to just be still. So I didn't feel the need to struggle, I just complied. I don't remember how long it lasted, but it seemed like within the hour or so, I was free to get up and move about. When I opened my eyes, to my surprise, lights were on everywhere. Ceiling fans were all on in the entire house, which was very weird because they were off when I laid down. I looked over, and Audie was sleeping soundly beside me.

My first thoughts were someone has been in our home, or perhaps were still there. "God help us," I whispered. I was led to get up and go into the kitchen area. The house appeared to be just the way I left it; with the exception of all the lights being on, everything looked perfect. It didn't feel right though. Something indeed was very wrong—I could sense it. I went back to wake up Audie. We both looked but couldn't find anything. All of a sudden, Audie calls my name. "Brenda! Oh my god, someone's been here. We've been robbed! Call the police."

I fell immediately to my knees and said, "Lord thank you for covering us! Thank you for your divine protection." I was so thankful for our lives having been spared. My purse had been stolen from the bedroom. The telephones, kitchen knives sets, wedding album, VCRs, and basically anything they could take immediately were stolen. I went back into the living room. All off a sudden, the wind blew slightly, and the patio door opened just a little. From there, we were able to track how they came in. They actually climbed over the back fence, trekked in the same way they went out using one set of foot prints to throw us off in thinking it was just one person when there were two.

When the policeman came to take the report, he asked if we knew anyone who might have wanted to harm us, if we had any knowledge of someone not liking us. We replied, "No, not to our knowledge no one." The policeman asked "Do you think it could have been your neighbors." We said, "We don't know. We just moved in and don't know our neighbors."

When we sensed that the police officer really wasn't taking the matter seriously, we began to pray and ask God for clarity of exactly what happened. The Holy Spirit said to take a credit card and use it on the back door to try to get in. I did so, and what do you know, it worked the first time. The police officer said they came in through the window, which wasn't the truth because the pane of the window was not broken, and the window was locked from inside the house. They came in through the back door as suspected by me and the Holy Spirit had instructed.

The screens on the windows were not cut and appeared to be loosened at best, but otherwise in good shape. This was clearly the work of a professional or someone who had access to the house before, perhaps with their own key. Like a builder or hired worker. Livid by now, I got in the car and drove around to the model homes and demanded to have the original key returned to me that day.

Through this situation, clearly the Lord showed me that having heeded the warning of having the house blessed even when others thought it was weird, uncool, unnecessary, unheard of, over the top.

I listened and obeyed God. To me, God showed the enemy even though he came in the middle of the night and stole material things from us and perhaps even wanted to take our lives. He couldn't because God had a protective hedge around us. The robbers could very well have the "material" things, but they could not touch me and Audie's souls, which belonged to God!

From there, the church family began to question our walk in Christ and asked us often about why we took our walk with Christ so seriously and does it really take all of that for us to serve God. I asked them why they didn't think that it took any effort at all on their part to serve God. They didn't appear to have taken their walk with Christ seriously. Honestly, is there any other way? And quite frankly right about now, I started to question why Audie and I were attending service there at all. Heaven forbid if we said "hallelujah" or "praise the Lord out loudly"; sometimes I almost feared for my safety.

Over the next several years, I continued to serve and obey God, and God continued to open more doors and make more ways for me and her family. Like the saying goes, for every new level, comes new devils. And boy oh boy did I not experience that first hand! When I tell you that people shun us with the exception of when it was time to "bless" them of course like with groceries, money for unexpected bills, and helping the church with building funds, etc. There was absolutely no hesitation in contacting the Murphy family or calling upon us to be a blessing to the body.

AN UNUSUAL ENCOUNTER PART 2

About a year or so before I left the church, a very well-known individual of the church who, at the time, lived in the neighborhood for years began to approach me with odd requests and comments. One day in particular, this individual said to me, "Sister Murphy, if I give you a gift, would you take it?" I thought that was rather odd, who does that? Usually if someone has a gift to present to a person, wouldn't they just give it to them?

One wouldn't think that it would have to come in the form of a trick question, would it? Should it come with strings attached, or are there? Anyway, right away, I noticed that this strange gift was given to me wrapped up in regular tissue paper not gift wrapping paper. After that episode, I started to feel very strangely in my body particularly in my lower back and legs area.

There were days, when I could hardly get in or out of bed, and I was only twenty-three years old at the time. The pain usually worsen on Saturday nights, and by Sunday mornings, the best I could do was lie down on the floor on my back and cry like a baby. It hurt to move or be touched. Audie took me from chiropractor to the best care the military base could offer, and they we often be met with no change in my overall health condition at the time. Test after test revealed nothing but more misery and pain ahead.

Over time, I was worn out with exhaustion, but I continued to seek the Lord. When I was able to attend church, I felt that an old spirit had invaded my body without my expressed permission. By now, I was thinking that I looked and acted old as well. Members would say, "Sister Murphy, are you okay? You look tired, are you sick? You are losing weight." Or depending upon who I was talking to, they would ask me if I was gaining weight. I was getting depressed because she I didn't understand what was happening to me.

Tired of being sick, one morning I called my eldest sister and told her about my personal situation and she instructed me on things that she could do to help my situation. I indeed followed the remedy and/or suggestions to the letter, and shortly thereafter, I received a letter from my sister with even more specific instructions. However, it was only until I received the letter that I began to really take notice of how others responded and treated me, which made me shocked, sad, and downright angry due to their suspicions.

I was at work one evening, and it was just about time for me to get off when a co-worker came in and said there was someone outside in the hallway waiting to see me. When I asked the co-worker what that individual's name was, they said, "They told me not to tell you. It's a surprise." Well, I never would have guessed it in a million years. When I entered the hallway, I did not see anyone at first. When I went toward the elevators, this woman was standing with her back to me. And though she looked familiar, I thought it cannot be true.

What is the likelihood of her coming to Texas without saying something to us first? I went up to the woman and said, "Excuse me, ma'am, are you looking for me?" When the individual turned around, she said, "Yes, I am." She hugged me with a beautiful and warm smile on her face.

I burst into tears right there in the hallway. In fact, I was so overwhelmed and grateful that she was there. It was my mother. I was full of questions and wondered about how, why, and when she had come. Most importantly, how did she get to my job, and who brought her there. On the way home, she filled me in with all the particulars: that my nephew and niece had actually gone to Mississippi, and they asked at the last minute if she would like to ride back with them for a surprise visit to see to me. And boy was I ever surprised.

Still curious about her unannounced trip, I probed more about why she was there. She just said, "Momma just missed her baby and wanted to see her babies that's all." For a brief moment, the interrogation stopped, and we just simply enjoyed every moment of her time being with us. We enjoyed my mom's cooking—everyday breakfast, lunch, and dinner. She made all kind of specialty dinners: chicken-n-dumplings, chicken-dressing, meatloaf, yams, potato salad. You name it, and her mom did that!

After being together for a couple of days, it was my mom's turn to ask the questions, and so she began by saying, "So, where is this church that you guys go to and are we going this week?" "Yes," I replied, "we're going to Bible study on Wednesday night."

Wednesday came, and we all got dressed as usual to go. I was so excited about introducing my mother to my church family. Interestingly enough, my mom seemingly took everything in about the church, including the drive on the way over there.

As she was being introduced to everyone, the individual who gave me the jewelry had yet to arrive, and church was almost beginning to start. About five to ten minutes before service began, in came the woman, and with a loud voice she said, "Well, looks like we have a visitor. Who might this be?" My mother stood and introduced herself with an outstretched hand. Looking her directly in the eyes, she said, "Hello, my name is Frances, and you are?"

Smiling or grinning as always, she said, "Well, my name is Harrietta, and I'll call you Little Big Murphy because you are Brenda's momma." My mother was not amused and told the woman so.

On the way home, my mother asked to see the "special gift" that this Harrietta person gave to me. I presented to her just as I had previously received it, still wrapped up in the tissue. After my mother received it, she immediate went to her room, closed the door, and we did not see or hear from her until the next morning for breakfast. She was rather quiet and reserved.

My mom looked like she had a lot on her mind. When they asked if she was okay, she said, "Yes, I think I am going to stay until the end of the week because Thanksgiving is Thursday, and I can leave either Friday or Saturday. Would that work for the both of you guys? We were extremely delighted, and without thought, said yes with big grins on our faces.

While backing out of the driveway one morning, the blinds to my mother's bedroom window was slightly opened, and we could see her down on her knees, praying with the tissue in her hand. As we were looking, I wondered what why she was praying over the gift that I received." I never questioned my mother about it all; I simply left it alone though I was extremely curious. That same evening, my mom asked if I had received any additional gifts and/or items from this same woman before, and as I thought about it, my reply was yes.

Little things like earrings, homemade cookies, scarves, etc. My mother's immediate reply was, "Well, do not take anything else from her. And do you still have those items such as the earrings? Have you ever worn them before?" Curious, I said, "No, I haven't they weren't my type.

After our Thanksgiving time together, my mom left that next day back to Mississippi. We missed her already, and she hadn't even gotten out of the state yet. We already felt the void and told her so. I could not put my finger on it, but I knew that my mom had actually come to visit us in particular on a special assignment from God, perhaps even to cover my life in prayer. I will never know all the details and maybe that is just as well.

When my mom got to Shreveport, as the bus stopped there as a fifteen-minute layover, my mom called us and talked about how proud she was of us and how much she enjoyed her stay. However, during our phone conversation, something interesting happened.

Apparently, someone approached my mother and said her ear-rings were pretty. My mother replied, "Oh, do you like them?" I could hear the woman saying, yes. My mom then said, "Here, you can have them along with this necklace and other stuff." The stranger thanked my mom, and they both said goodbye.

Shocked, I said "Mom, who was that you were talking to?" She said, I don't know, baby, that was just some nice woman I met while in the bathroom, and she liked the earrings that I brought from your house that you didn't like. Oh, by the way, I also took other jewelry your friend from the church gave you. Harrietta, is that her name? You don't mind, do you?" In disbelief and maybe even partially relieved, I said, "No, ma'am."

Not knowing what to really make of any of it. I decided to pray and ask God to cover me. Now, I was scared for sure, I knew in my heart something was terribly wrong. I just could not put my finger on it. As I continued to attend this same church from time to time, Sister Harrietta as she was well known would approach me and inquire about how my mother was doing, and in particu-larly, what my mother thought about her. Needless to say I told her mom was fine. No comment about how she really felt about her though, if you know what I mean.

About two months after this episode, my back started to bother me again, and this time, the pastor's wife approached me and said, "Sister Murphy, have you been to the doctor about your back problems because it seems to me that something more is wrong. You are too young to be having this many back problems. I want you to go get checked out." I didn't necessarily go to the doctor because she said so, but I did go because the pains had suddenly come back with a vengeance, and I felt I had no other choice. Now Audie and I were both scared and worried. I cried a lot and prayed even more.

This time when I went to the doctor, they reviewed my records and sent me to a "specialist" who was from Nigeria. After exam-ining me, the doctor said, "Ma'am, I can assure you this is not a kidney problem, bladder infection, or anything like that. It seems more like a specific problem that is contributing to your pain. In my country, we see this all the time."

The doctor provided me with a specific medicine and sent me on my way. That was enough to convince me right then and there that something seriously was wrong. I dove more into prayer, this time incorporating fasting as I knew to do. I continued to pray until there were answers and breakthroughs in my life. In my opinion, my life was on the line, and I needed answers quickly.

Thankfully, I believed that God sent an angel in my life named Sister Charmaine. The interesting thing was that as long as I had been a member of this particular church, at best, I may have held a personal conversation at least three times with this individual. Yet in this instance, God was using Sister Charmaine to be a blessing to me at this important time in my life.

Charmaine informed me that she would be calling me tonight around 6:00 pm to give me some vital information that would serve as a benefit to me and she wanted to make sure that I would be available. All the way home I pondered what in the world is all of this about.

Audie, who was driving, finally chimed in and said to my otherwise one-woman conversation, "Bren, don't worry. I am sure whatever it is, she'll tell you when she talks to you, relax." My thoughts were, sure, this ain't your life on the line; at about 5:45 p.m., I all but begged Audie to come in the bedroom with me when Sister Charmaine called because I didn't want to be alone to endure the telephone conversation.

I felt that I needed massive moral support. At exactly 6:00 p.m., my telephone ranged. Nervously I answered, trying to appear strong when I was a nervous wreck, strong in Christ, worthless in the flesh right about now. Answering the phone, I said, "Hello, Sister Charmaine, how are you?"

She immediately replied, "I'm fine, Sister Murphy. I've got something very important to tell you, and I am going to need for you to pay close attention to every detail. You are not to repeat anything that I am going to say. You are not to approach the people that I am going to mention in this conversation about any of this, or I will totally deny telling you any of it."

I almost squeezed the life out of Audie's hand. She began by saying, "There are at least two people who attend our church that absolutely hate you. Not dislike, not disapprove, they hate you to the point where they want to do bodily harm to you, but not in the visible way in which you may imagine but in other ways. They watch you constantly and are very jealous of how you carry yourself—from your dress to the influence that you have with others, your speech and favor, right down to your marriage and your home. "They think that you have an easy life and lifestyle. You are too holy, you are talented and gifted. Even though they smile in your face, they cannot stand you and strive every day to make your life miserable. They offer you things even though you do not need them. You take them just to be polite. Stop that immediately. Do not take anything else from anyone at any time. They watch your every move and even notice where you sit to you having a habit of taking off your shoes while singing in the choir. Stop that as of now. You must become very guarded from this time forward."

She described both of the women to the letter. I knew instantly both of their names and full description in the spirit. Crying profusely, I started immediately asking God how people could be so evil especially since I had not done anything but well, and yet they hated me to the point of hurt and evilness.

Charmaine continued to talk and advised me to pay close attention because this would be the first and last conversation she and I would have concerning this topic. Charmaine said, "When you see them in church, you are to simply greet them with a smile, no hugs, and kisses on the cheeks or any touchy-feely emotion. Do not show resentment, anger, malice, or fear.

God has it all in control. This conversation is strictly to let you know that you have enemies in close range and to not be ignorant of the fact." With that, she hung up. That was the first and last conversation we ever had regarding the same. In church, she simply greeted me as she always did, smile, wave, and said "Hi, Sister Murphy."

Other than that, nothing else, Charmaine provided not a grin, a goodbye, or anything. I was truly grateful that she had allowed God to use her in such a way that my personal prayers had been answered. It was very difficult for me to continue attending church and pretending not knowing what had taken place with these women, but God guided me through it all.

At the end of the month, Shelley, the younger woman, had the audacity to approach me. Smiling, she handed me this old, wrinkled, greasy, smelly, and beyond used paper bag all rolled down in her hand. The woman looked me directly in the eyes and said, "Here, I have something for you." Honestly, my first thoughts, Were oh really, and I have something for you. My fist right between your eyes!

I extended my hand and took it, barely touching the bag as though it was discarded trash, which is what it truly amounted to be. Immediately after taking the paper bag, I drove directly to the trash bin and dumped it. On that following Friday night, just like every other night, I took my hot bath and got ready for bed, pretty much always leaving Audie up to watch whatever particular sport that was on television that evening.

Sometime before the morning, I remembered it vividly a vision that the Lord showed me. I was awakened only to see myself still in the bedroom asleep; however, it appeared that the ceiling was missing from our bedroom. I was sitting above my bed with my feet hanging down from the ceiling, looking down into our bedroom. I could see all over our house, including watching both Audie and I asleep in bed.

All of a sudden, I could hear our front door close, and this specific sound came down the hallway into our bedroom. The puppy appeared to be distinct in size, snow white in color, and had beautiful captivating eyes. It donned a pink bow in the center of her head. In other words, harmless or so it seemed.

Upon entering the bedroom, the little puppy immediately scurries over to my side of the bed and sat down at the corner never, taking its eyes off of me. From my perspective, it appeared as though the puppy was staring at me for some specific reason. I remembered seeing myself awake, as if someone had touched me, and I sat straight up in the bed and noticed the puppy being there in my presence.

When I spoke to the puppy, I said, "Heah, what are you doing in here, how did you get in here?" The puppy simply just looked at me, panting as dogs do. When all of a sudden, the puppy moved up closer to the bed where I was sitting up, and just then, I could sense the puppy about to jump up onto the bed when I screamed, "Stop and get out."

The puppy appeared to become extremely angry and agitated, and now began barking at me. The more I yelled for the puppy to get out the bedroom, the angrier the puppy became. It began turning around in circles; the barks becoming more vicious. This scared me, and I tried to awaken Audie, but he just rolled back and forth in the bed, never waking up. I pushed him as if he were a dead man without him ever making any sounds at all. After my third attempt to awake him, I heard this voice saying, "Don't turn away from the dog. Stay focused."

I did just that, but while doing so, I noticed the once seemingly cute and innocently looking puppy with each turn he made was changing before my very eyes. The puppy began to grow taller and taller and his mouth began to grow wider and larger from its original state. The now dog began to make what seemed like a growling noise that only large dogs make. His teeth were long and pointy. The dog's eyes blazed and the dog was now starring deeply into my eyes. I realized this was no longer a regular dog but perhaps a wolf.

I opened my mouth realizing that I was now in for the fight of my life, I said, "Jesus, Jesus, help me! The blood of Jesus!" About the third time I called on the name of Jesus, I heard this enormous pop that caused me to jump seemingly out of my skin. The puppy/wolf-like dog had vanished but not with-out a struggle. As I looked down at myself, I realized that my entire gown was now drenched in sweat. My hair matted to my head, and I was shaking uncontrollably.

I remembered this very loud ringing noise in my ear, and it was my alarm clock going off at exactly 6:00 a.m. Looking over at Audie, I noticed that he was still sound asleep. He had not heard, seen, or witnessed a thing. I was absolutely stunned. At the time, we had a dog who was a chow mixed with shepherd in the back-yard. He was going nuts, barking and barking, so I jumped up, ran around the bed into the bathroom, which had a rather large window.

As I pulled back the blinds and opened the window to yell at Garth, which was the dog's name, I saw with my own eyes the bite that had been taken out of our backyard fence. Now, not literally, but spiritually speaking. And Garth was running up and down the backyard, barking and barking at this same spirit that I had just witnessed in our house.

The minute I called Garth's name, he stopped barking and turned around to acknowledge me. I rubbed my eyes, making sure that I had truly witnessed this incredible sight; when all of a sudden, that particular fence disappeared. I sat down in the middle of my bathroom floor and cried my heart out. I said, "Lord, what is happening to me? What is really going on?"

At first, I did not mention anything to Audie for fear that he would think that I was truly losing it or making it all up. I felt so alone and isolated. I wanted desperately to run and hide. The problem was, where to? The only safe place was under the shadow of the mighty, and I was for sure already there in order to survive what I had in fact just witnessed.

Eventually, feeling more comfortable with what had taken place, I told Audie about what I had experienced. He looked shocked, nervous, and concerned about me and the incident. Although he had firsthand knowledge about what I had been going through, he could not get a pulse on what, when, or why. He held me and prayed for the both of us. I was not ashamed in saying that up until now, I had never in my life experienced anything like this before, and I prayed that I never would again.

Not knowing what to do next, I decided not to tell anyone about it. Not my pastor, family, friends, or coworkers—absolutely no one else needed to know. Over the next three to six months, I continued to fast, pray, and watch God bring all of this to past. One Sunday morning, during Sunday school, I was up to teach and shared my testimony.

After teaching Sunday school that morning, much to my surprise, Sister Harrietta met with me afterward and asked me point-blank, "Is the person who you were speaking about in class the one in the vision?"

Catching me totally by surprise, I turned to Harrietta and said, "I really don't know. It was a black wolf disguised to look like an innocent puppy coming to harm me, is that what you consider yourself to be?

With that being said, Harrietta hurriedly put on her choir rob and disappeared into the choir stand. Now, being armed with the truth of God, I felt that I now knew what to look for. The barraged array of questions as what, when, where, and why no longer plagued me. All I cared about right now was being covered under the wings of the Almighty God and that my family was being protected.

My pastor and I were pretty close, and when I shared the vision personally, he literally hung his head and cried like an infant. He told me that his congregation had been plagued with certain issues in the past and that there had been many people who had been hurt and left the church due to certain member's involvement before. When I looked into the pastor's eyes, I realized the tears were not from mere shock of my words, but of familiarity of times past that has quite possibly resurfaced for more vengeance.

ANOTHER LEVEL OF FAITH

As time passed, Audie was eventually moved to San Antonio because the Fort Worth military base station closed. The news of the base closing was stressing for everyone—military families, merchants, churches, and the community at large. Wanting to make the right decision about our family and the house, we continued to pray and ask God for directions of what and where and what the next move for us would be spiritually, physically, and financially.

Audie was stationed in San Antonio about six months prior to my moving. You can only imagine how stressful that move was on the both of us. Up until now, we had never been separated and were not use to doing things or making decisions separately. Because of the closing of the base, military housing was extremely scarce. Audie pretty much had to take whatever was left, which meant not too much of anything. In fact, Audie ended up living off base, undergirding all costs—the apartment, all utilities and purchasing a second car. At that moment, life was very tasking.

In the end, we both decided that he would move to San Antonio without me because the bases were closing sooner than first mentioned. We were also not prepared to sell our house or place it on the market and to move to San Antonio cold turkey within a few months. Even though our decision to live apart was difficult, we realized it was the best for us in that particular moment. Up until that time, we had not told any of our family, including my mom and dad, about our final decision because we did not want to worry them.

In the beginning, we tried to stick to our promise of visiting each other every weekend. However, slowly but surely funds our funds got tight, and we slowed down to every other weekend; eventually, even once a month, which was becoming even more cumbersome and a major challenge. It was just too much. At the time, I worked for a law firm, and I was considered the office manager for three attorneys dumb, dumber, and dumbest. It seemed like the harder I was willing to work, the less they wanted to pay me.

At this particular law firm, everything was very fast-paced clients coming and going, cases being won and lost. One never could tell. One particular event that I remembered the most was telling one of my bosses that my husband had moved to San Antonio due to restructuring of the military base, and that I would be joining him hopefully soon at some point.

During this process, for the past eight years now, Audie and I would go home and spend Thanksgiving with my parents and attend my dad's annual Thanksgiving musical at the church. We always looked forward to hearing this particular group sings and going shopping with my parents the next day which was very important to my parents.

Even though things were extremely difficult for me and Audie during these first several months, we knew in our hearts that we still wanted to go home and spend that time with family as we had done time and time again during the holidays. So we pooled our little resources together and just went for it. No one in our immediate family knew just how under the gun we really were, and we wouldn't dare share it with anyone either.

Thanksgiving and the musical were just wonderful as the previous years. We enjoyed every moment of it. However after service, a pastor walked up to me and asked if he could have a word with me. Knowing him for some years back and feeling quite comfortable with speaking with him, I smiled and said yes. Taking me to the side, the pastor said, "Now, I know this may sound a little strange at first, but I want you to just listen.

Nervous about it all but agreeing to comply, I was eager to hear what he had to say. He began by saying, "You are going to be moving the first part or no later than the second month of next year." He said, "Don't worry. Don't worry about a thing. God wants you to know that He has it all in control. When you get to your new location, your place of where you will be staying is already taken care of. Your job and church home has already been picked out for you. Don't worry about anything.

In fact tonight, when you get home, begin reading Proverbs 3:5. *"Trust in the Lord with all your heart and lean not unto your own understanding."* Continue reading the entire chapter and just bear into that scripture depending upon God for everything." I tried desperately not to cry, but the tears broke free anyway and I began streaming down my face. Thank you Lord Jesus!

On the drive back home, everyone else was laughing and talking about the musical. All the while, I continued to rejoice and cry, celebrating what God had spoken in my ear through His servant. I was thankful that the car was dark and no one had noticed me.

Once the trip was over and Audie was back in San Antonio, I was alone without family and real friends. I prayed to God daily to give me the strength and the necessary courage to finish my personal course. Finally, it was December, and I could kind of breathe a breath of fresh air. I decided to tell my boss about Audie being moved to San Antonio and that I in fact definitely would soon be joining him.

At first, my bosses all seemed to be shocked, a little sad and asked what they could do to get me to stay until the end of the month at least. I really liked and worked well with the owner of the law firm, David. He was elderly and had a lot of wisdom. Most importantly, he knew how to treat others, which was extremely important to me. On the other hand, Mr. Carpenter, the partner, was just a straight-up nutcase without the shell. He was always biting off more than he could chew.

Taking on court cases that he was ill-prepared for and just needed to earn his dues just like the next person before launching out into the deep with no real direction. Even still, after the meeting, Mr. Carpenter approached me and begged me to stay until the end of the year, promising that he would one give me a pay raise to do so. He also promised me that I would be able to take every Friday off to go to San Antonio to spend a nice long weekend with my husband.

Needless to say, none of that ever came to fruition; in fact, the workload increased dramatically. It was a month before Christmas, and typically within the office all the secretaries usually received a Christmas bonus of a minimum of one thousand dollars with no tax deduction each. So naturally, I was thinking privately, thank God because my family could sure use that extra money for bills.

As our offices planned for the Christmas party, the owner of the law firm travelled a lot, and as tradition would have it, he went out of town for the holidays, leaving dumber in charge to make sure everything ran smoothly. Well, dumber decided to take matters into his own hands and told me what he thought of me on Christmas Eve. He also made sure that I would not attend the Christmas party due to extra work that had to be done he said at the last minute although all the other offices were shut down for the day.

You see dumber was one of those types of individuals that felt that everyone, including his immediate family, should bow down to him. He truly felt that he was superior to all those around him and when he said jump, one need only ask, "How high?" Listening to him provide his personal version of why I didn't deserve a raise from him, he asked me what I thought about his comments.

Even though I was hurt, angry, and disappointed that I would not be receiving the bonus I knew I deserved, I simply said to him, "No, I don't have anything to say other than I do not agree with the comments you had to say about me at all. And at the end of the day, it's your money, and you may spend it any way you choose. If you feel that I do not deserve a bonus from you, then you do well to keep it. I will survive." Wouldn't you know it, he became even more upset and ranted some more.

He then told me that I had to work until 5:00 p.m. before I could leave to go home that day. Everyone else in the entire building had already left right after the yearly scheduled Christmas luncheon at 1:00 p.m. and would not be back until one week later. I went back to my desk after the onslaught of insults and prayed that I would not cry and continued to work.

I could feel the presence of God over me in that moment. Shocked that I was still there and working, he eventually crawled out of his miserable little hole and approached my desk, and said, "That's okay, you can go home now." I didn't bother to give him my personal attention at all and kept typing. He said again, "Did you hear me? I said that you can go home now." I turned to Lucifer and said, "I heard you loud and clear.

However, since you are paying me to do my job, no matter how unskilled you say I am, I am going to finish what I started until 5:00 p.m. so that I will not be in your debt for anything." He stared at me, sat in front of my desk, put his hands up to his cheeks and asked, "Brenda, what is wrong with you? Why aren't you angry, cursing, or walking out? Did you not understand what I just said to you? See, that's your problem, you don't ever get upset. You just take whatever people say to you without fighting back."

I said to him, "See that's where you and I totally disagree. You think that I need to spend my time trying to convince you of my personal worth and value when I already know who and whose I am whether or not I get a bonus check or a regular check or one red cent from this law firm. My personal worth is not hidden or connected to this place of business, or you for that matter. And as far as not responding back to you in a negative, fretful, chaotic, or argumentative way, I usually deem comments for those types of conversations that truly have no real merit or truth as being virtually useless and I choose not to respond at all.

Now, if you will please excuse me for being rude, I still owe you according to the time clock another fifteen minutes before 5:00 p.m." And I continued to type out my daily reports.

He got his briefcase and left, slamming the door behind him. I finished my work, locked up as usual, and talked to God about it all the way home. That Sunday, I went to church with some close friends. During the service, their pastor called me up to the front of the church and prophesied to me that God said that He had seen my struggles, hurts, treatment of others, and that he was working it all out for my good and on my behalf. That was all I needed to know and believe.

When I returned to work, Mr. Carpenter had a check of $325.00 laid out on his desk with my name on it. Not only did I leave the check in the same spot, I decided to just work all around it. For days, he didn't say anything, and neither did I about the check.

Finally, he couldn't take it anymore and called me into his office. When I went in, he asked me in a rather stern voice, "Why is this still laying here?"

"What do you mean?" I replied.

"This check with your name on it?"

"As far as I can tell, it's the last place where you laid it on your desk."

"Didn't you see your name on it?"

"Yes, sir," I replied. "I also recognized that you knew where my desk was also. And if you really wanted me to have it before or after Christmas, when everyone else received their bonus during the holidays in their hands from their boss's during lunch, you would have made an effort to do the same with me, and when that didn't happen, I did not think that it was my place to automatically assume that you meant for me to simply take a check off your desk simply because it had my name on it without your knowledge or consent."

With that, I removed myself from his office and went back to my desk. He followed in pursuit. He asked me to forgive him and that he was just upset about some personal things going on in his life and to take the check. I still didn't take it until the day was over. The life lesson I learned that day was, though man tried to slay me, yet even the more would I trust in God Almighty because if I didn't realize it before, I was beginning to understand that all my help was coming directly from the Lord and not man.

Not wanting him to know that I didn't have any money, I humbly declined the offer. Of course, I very much so wanted to go home to San Antonio so I could see my hubby.

Believing that the opportunity had passed me by, I was saddened by it but tried not to show it in my disposition or voice. What I didn't realize was at the end of my shift that evening, as we were both leaving the office, my coworker once again said, "Heah, girl, I am so glad that I caught you before you left.

You're still riding with me, right?" With tears in my eyes, I reminded her that I didn't have any money to offer her for gas and that I would have to decline the offer. She said, "Please, get your packing together, and I will pick you on Friday morning. Don't even think about going to work. You're always going in. Call him and let him know you will see him on Monday. He'll be alright."

I gave the coworker my address and telephone number, and she picked me up on Friday like clockwork. As I was leaving the house, I heard this voice within my spirit say, "Don't forget to pack a blouse and heels." I turned around, went back into the house, grabbed a beautiful skirt and heels, and the rest was history. I thoroughly enjoyed the trip and the company all the way to San Antonio. We made it by 12:00 p.m., just in time for lunch.

Audie met me at the door, and he was excited to see me. He was making breakfast for two. Boy, did I ever miss his down home cooking. To my surprise, he encouraged me to check out the newspaper, particularly the help wanted section. He also told me that he had been sending out resumes on my behalf. Ironically, while eating breakfast, I spotted this little bitty tiny ad in the paper for a legal secretary in Castle Hills, which is near the airport. Nervously, I decided to call the number listed and spoke with a woman who identified herself as Mary. After speaking with her on the phone, she encouraged me to come right on over and gave me the address.

Explaining to her that I was very new in town, to my surprise she still welcomed me to come anyway. So I did, and after arriving at the law firm, I was greeted nicely and given an application to be completed on the spot.

There were additional tests to take and an extended interview process by the founder of the law firm, as well as a brief tour and meeting the staff. It felt really great. We celebrated in advance. On Sunday evening, my friend and I headed back home to Fort Worth. I told my coworker about our adventure, and the coworker said, "Well, I am glad that everything worked out for you and that you decided to make the trip with me even though this will be your first and last trip with me before you start working in San Antonio at your new job!"

I was extremely shocked and looked at my coworker with my mouth completely opened. She then said, "Um-hum, I said it. Honey, that job is yours. You just watch and see." On Tuesday morning after getting in to the office, my boss was his usual unprofessional self, once again reneging on a promise to allow me to work longer hours through the week so that I could take Friday's off to go to San Antonio to look for a job.

Well, those magic moments never materialized. Looking back, I realized that perhaps I should have never ever entertained kindness from the enemy when there was no good thing that resided in him, at least not near the surface area.

Nevertheless, I thought, God doesn't need my enemies to bless me. He alone is God all by himself! About 9:30 a.m. on Wednesday morning, my phone ranged. It was Mary, the office manager from the law firm, asking me whether or not I was still interested in the job. The first thing I thought about was Pastor Maxwell's prophecy to me.

Instantly I started smiling and couldn't stop. For fear of people inadvertently walking into the firm and finding me grinning like a Cheshire cat, I hurriedly agreed to take the job! Mary said that I would need a reference and asked to speak to my boss.

Thankfully he was on the phone with a client, and I asked her if there was another person she could speak with. She confirmed that any manager or lawyer in the office would suffice. Praise the Lord for small favors! I had just the right person in mind, and he was "human" with compassion. It's funny how God will use whomever he chooses to bless you even if they don't know why they are doing you a favor personally.

The man that gave me a glowing reference was someone who barely spoke to me; however, his secretary and I were close at the time, and she could not stand my boss and desired to see me move forward. Well, come to think of it, very few people in or out of the office could or would for that matter tolerate my boss.

After the call was passed to the other attorney for a reference check, he came over to my desk within five minutes to meet with my boss for lunch. After they all left the building, he pretended to have left something behind and came back and said, "Brenda, don't worry. I not only gave you a glowing reference but I also told them how lucky they will be to have you as a part of their team."

Eager to see my snookums, I instantly said yes that would take the job. I quickly called Audie and told him that I was coming for the weekend. He was eagerly excited about the whole thing. Our weekends together were always wonderful, and we drove around trying to learn more about San Antonio.

Sunday came too fast, and now I was on my way back home. Now the next thing on the agenda was whether or not to sell or put the house up for rent. Together we prayed about it and within a couple of days, an old friend called me. I mentioned that I would be moving to San Antonio but needed to rent/sell our home while we were away.

The friend asked how much and for how long would we be away. I told her for at least six months to a year. We discussed it further and met with the friend and the deal was done. We began to pack and get ready for our next adventure. The friend moved in, and we moved out. When we thought about it, just like the pastor had previously stated, God had indeed answered my prayers, and I was sure those of Audie's as well.

I really loved everything about San Antonio—the food, the people, church, and even the heat. My time there was great. I grew under the wonderful wings of the Almighty. I was introduced to other women who loved God and worshipped him with sincerity and without fanfare. They were ordinary yet trusting, hopeful, loving, and extremely thoughtful people. The women often met for Bible study in different homes or locations every weekend. They celebrated each other victories and also shared in the others valleys as well. No stone was ever left unturned.

Through various meetings, these women introduced me to an all-women's Bible study group called Bible Study for Females (BSF). It was worth every minute of my time. I looked forward to attending the sessions and eagerly did my homework with the anticipation of sharing my answers or responses in class. I was growing spiritually by major leaps and bounds, and there was no place I'd rather be than in the presence of my Lord.

GETTING THE JOB

The job at the law firm was okay. However, like any other job, it had it perks and lows. Up to this point, it seemed that every job I ever gotten wanted my blood and then some. This boss was no different. Well, he was a little eccentric. For instance, his number one rule was if you brought your lunch and left it in the refrigerator to eat later, chances were you would not be able to find it because he would have already done the honors.

Everything on the premises of that law firm belonged to him, and if he wanted to eat it, he could and he would. He was also very racist, but of course he didn't see himself as being such. He was the equivalent of an Archie Bunker type of individual in deep denial about certain things in life; great attorney, horrible mannerisms. Oh, well, I guess you can't have it all.

My boss was a person whom I would consider to be very paranoid. He would put all of his workload in numerical order, and if anything—and I mean anything—was taken out of sequence, he would become immediately infuriated over the least tiny insignificant thing.

After being employed at this law firm for over a year, I learned that whenever he had a problem with any of his employees, he always threatened to fire them on the spot. He would shout, "Just get out of my office," often with little or no warning whether he was right or wrong.

Whether it was his fault or not, he never apologized for anything; he made working for him almost unbearable and very stressful. Thankfully, his type of behavior was not just shared among his employees, but was often noticed with his family members as well, especially his wife. They were known to have a couple of weekly office brawls in the open for all to see and witness, and then the next five to ten minutes were spent kissing and making up. Jesus, take the wheel!

One night after going home from work, Audie had to go out of town on business to St. Louis, Missouri, and I was home alone for the week. Usually, when I got off work, I would be mentally drained and stressed from all the unnecessary challenges and drama any day could bring. On the way home, I decided to stop by the restaurant and grabbed a bite to eat, take a hot bath, eat, and go to bed.

Some time that night, I once again had a vision about being near my original church location where I grew up. I was standing in the middle of this gravel road, and to my left was this really woodsy area filled with trees, like a forest. To my right were a ditch and a little church that sat on the other side of the road. The reality of it all is that the original place is just like that even now.

Anyway, behind the little church stood a tall corporate building, almost sharing the same yard space. The corporate building was burning from the outside, and people were running, screaming for help. Meanwhile, the church was fine, and the service continued uninterrupted despite all the commotion going on. All of a sudden, this fire truck appeared out of nowhere with its engine lights flashing. The fire truck didn't appear to be in a rush but rather approached the fire burning building at a normal rate of speed.

When the driver got out of the vehicle, he was dressed in beautiful white linen attire. He was wearing woven sandals like the biblical days. His skin was radiant, perfect in tone, and his eyes were pure and extremely bright. He spoke no audible words, yet I fully understood our conversation. His eyes pierced straight through my very soul. I could feel the invasion, but I was not fearful at all.

He gathered the water hose from the truck, stepped over the little ditch, and went in the building in what seemed like seconds before the fire from the corporation was put out. When he got out, he suddenly turned to me and said, "Don't worry. I will send you help." He got into his truck and slowly turned around and went on his way with his arm out of the window and whistling as he drove away in the opposite direction. When I woke the next morning, the stress of my job was no more. I didn't have that same anxiety and dread that I was accustomed to experiencing before I went into work every morning. There was no fear at all.

The next day, Mary asked me out to lunch. The problem was her car was in the shop, and the truth of the matter was she was hungry and wanted to go out. So she asked me if I wanted to go with her, especially since I was the one driving. Over lunch, Mary wasted no time in asking me how I was doing, and what did I dream about last night. While I thought immediately it was a strange question to be asked by anyone, I wasted no time sharing.

Mary absolutely loved to eat and thoroughly enjoyed every morsel of her food, even the crumbs on the plate. But this time, as I was telling her about my vision, she stopped midair from biting into her sandwich. Her skin turned white as a ghost, and her mouth was wide open. "What? Are you some kind of a prophet?" Mary pushed back from the table, gathered her food, and said, "Let's go." Remember, she is riding with me, and we had just sat down to eat.

It was obvious that she was perturbed, and everyone in the restaurant could tell by the look on her face. I didn't want to cause any additional drama and simply got my purse, a to-go box, and exited the building gracefully. Not understanding what just happened, I tried to press for more information in the car. Mary was mum all the way back to work. She said nothing just looking out of the window until we got back to work. As soon as the car stopped, she got out and walked ahead of me and went straight into her office.

I thought to myself, Is this woman crazy? Within an hour, she sent an e-mail blast that she was resigning from her position effective immediately. She then called her daughter and asked her to come and pick her up as she was packing and had just given her boss her notice. To say he was shocked and taken aback was an understatement.

In fact, our entire office didn't see it coming. When he probed her for more information, he discovered through files and billing statements that she had been stealing large sums of money from the business. She was giving the creditors my name and others within the firm as the fall guy should her secret ever surface.

Our boss told me that Mary was always telling him negative things about me behind my back, and he thought that I was unhappy and didn't like my job based upon the lies she was telling him behind the entire staff's back. Yet in our faces, she was always smiling and calling everyone darling and sweetheart. This is a woman our boss trusted to be office manager for seven years, and she had been deceiving his firm almost immediately after employment. Thank God for the vision and thank him for his divine protection.

TRUSTING GOD NO MATTER WHAT

"Look to the Lord and his strength; seek his face always."
—Psalms 105:4 (NIV)

The day finally came for me and Audie to move back to Fort Worth. I was not happy about the move at all. For the very first time, I spiritually felt like my life had meaning and was on solid ground again. I was growing by leaps and bounds, I enjoyed the fellowship of the other women, and I was being used by God. Most importantly, I was happy with my life. Now, the very thought of moving back at this particular time in my life was just not cutting it for me.

Audie and I had gotten news that Brooks Air Force Base would be closing down as well, and we would eventually have to move back to Fort Worth. Audie decided to retire and just serve the rest of his time in reserves. It was a wonderful and beautiful ceremony. The flag was flown on my birthday, and Audie received full honors. Once again, I was extremely proud of him. Audie was looking forward to coming back to Fort Worth. Honestly I could not see the vision and often told him so still I was willing to make it work for my family's sake.

By now I was becoming more conscious of my words and giving them power and influence in my life. I knew that my words could be used for positive or negative reactions and that what I allowed to flow through my mouth would become my outcome.

I realized if I were not careful each day, I could start to live my life with a self-absorb, condescending motive. In my past, I could easily look back and see how I had allowed the enemy to destroy my day through my own actions by always starting my day and sometimes ending my day with crazy words that went something like this: "I don't care who likes me. I don't need them." When deep down inside, I really hoped someone would finally see and embrace the fact that I did care about how others saw me and, more importantly, how God saw me.

In the weeks of preparation of moving back to Fort Worth, I was on my way to the church for midweek services. I was running late. While in the parking lot, I was almost in the car when this voice called out to me: "Miss, can you please help me to the bus stop?" I didn't pay the person any attention and proceeded to enter my car, and once again, he said it. "Heah miss, could you please help me find the bus stop?" I was hoping and praying that he was not talking to me, but of course as luck would have it, he was.

Very reluctantly I approached the gentleman but was not too sure if I should or not, he was walking with a cane and appeared to be blind. I wasn't falling for it I needed proof that he actually was. So I waived my hands in front of his eyes. I made funny faces and poked my tongue out. When I was really convinced that he was blind, I asked how I could help him. He said, "I need to find the bus stop. Can you please help me?" Once across the street at the bus stop, I figured my job was done and turned to walk away.

Little did I know, it had all been a set-up. The man starts to minister to me. I turned and said, "Say what?" He asked me a series of questions, things like my name, was I married, why I didn't want to move back to Fort Worth. After a while, I was intrigued by his demeanor and humbleness. By now, I was no longer fearful but rather pulled into his space and wanted to investigate more, so I stayed.

He told me that God had a calling on my life, and the specifics of that call to a degree. He further informed me that I would not regret the work that God had in store for me, and I should indeed return home. I listened and followed suit, and I never looked back since.

THE MOVE BACK TO FORT WORTH

After moving back to Fort Worth, I had another particular vision. I used that word because I knew the difference between visions and dreams, and there is a big difference between the two. This vision would take me back to when I lived in Detroit. However, during the vision, I had already moved to Texas and was going back home to visit some old friends.

In the vision, I called my sister Vera and informed her that I would be coming back and asked Vera if she could pick me up from the airport when I arrived. Of course, she said yes and did so. When I told my sister about my purpose for coming, she became very sad and tried her best to discourage me from doing so. Nevertheless, I still made the trip. Vera reluctantly dropped me off at the so-called friend's house and drove away.

Eager to see those I recalled at the time as my friends, I ranged their door bell and waited for someone to open the door. Finally, the door opened, but the person who answered did not stick around to personally greet me at all. They simply opened the door and walked away, leaving me to come in at own leisure.

Feeling the uninvited welcome, I felt at this point, I had no choice but to enter into the house or be left standing alone on the front porch. After doing so, I called out my friend's name; to my surprise, there were others there in the house as well. The room was not very well lighted, so I could just make out who I thought they were. At first, I was curious as to why they would not come out of this particular room to talk with me, especially after I had come such a long way to be with them and the trip was planned by all of us.

After a couple of hours of noticeable strange events, I felt very uncomfortable and wanted to leave. When I decided to do so, I noticed that no one appeared to care one way or the other. So I stood up and made my way to the front door of what appeared to be an apartment. However, after I had reached the front door and got outside, I noticed that it had been raining. I looked for my purse to get some change for the bus. That's when I noticed that my entire purse was missing—the only thing I had remaining was the purse strap. I had been robbed while visiting those that claimed to be my friend.

I was not sure when any of that happened in the apartment. I was distraught and didn't know what to do. I started crying and wondering what had I gotten myself into. As I was visibly upset, I heard this very soothing and comforting voice that seemed to be coming out of nowhere. I looked around and saw this huge woman with the most perfect complexion and gorgeous white teeth. She said to me, "What's wrong?"

Startled, I said, "I want to go home, but I have no money or a purse. I think that I have been robbed." The woman replied, "Meet me in the streets, and I'll help you." Reluctantly, I followed her lead and did so. However, the strangest thing happened when I did. Once I met her in the streets, the scene changed from Detroit as I knew it to an even more familiar place. It was the road right outside of my old front door where I grew up, so I knew the area quite well.

I met the woman there in the streets, and the woman stood behind me, dwarfing me in stature. I was amazed just how tall and big this individual was up close and personal. The woman continued to instruct me on the way home, or at least out of my current situation. She showed me this book that was definitely not the norm. It was enormous.

During the woman's instructions to me, she said that it would be imperative that I made my "journey" within fifteen minutes that sixteen minutes was too late and fourteen minutes would be too early. Fifteen minutes is exactly what had been allotted to me to arrive at my destination. The woman tore a page out of this gigantic book, folding it in a particular manner, and stretched the palm of my hand opened. She placed the neatly folded page in my hand and once again stood directly behind me on a little hill. She said, "Do you see where you are going?"

I replied, "Yes, primarily because I grew up there and knew the area well. However, I could not see the end of the journey in its entirety on this particular day due to it being heavily lined with lots of trees that were budding in that area; therefore making it challenging for me to see clearly to my appointed destination.

Eager to go home, I complied with her wishes and looked forward to the journey at hand. With that statement, she gave me a little shove and said, "Go my, daughter." I started running down this hill into the gravel road, which was challenging to say the least. Along the way, I could feel this ungodly energy or pressure making horrific noises barreling in hot pursuit of my demise. I really didn't need to turn around to see what was behind me because I could already sense it was evil. So I ran as fast as I could without turning around.

When I first started the "journey" home, I ran with confidence, slow but assured. However, I noticed that when I sensed imminent danger, I quickly surrendered and started to run out of control because I felt that my very life was at stake. I was crying profusely as my heart began to beat faster and faster; I was sweating and extremely nervous. I cried out to God with all that I had within me.

This force of evil was gaining on me, and I knew in my spirit that it was designed to kill me. Not cripple me, hurt me, damage me, but kill me. Everything about it said so. When the presence of this force reached the side of me, I heard a voice that said, "Brenda, look at it."

I immediately said no. I didn't want to and I kept running as fast as my legs would take me. Not only did I run out of order, but I deemed myself as having already lost the battle for my life and was simply bracing myself for the inevitable.

The spirit said again, but with more definition, "I said, look at it." This time it was not meant as a polite suggestion but rather more of a command. This time, frightened, feeling defeated, overwhelmed, and scared for my life, I looked up into the face of a beast that was so hideous and ugly until he reeked of evil firsthand. He was three-parted. The feet of this beast was hoofed; his legs and thighs were extremely muscular with very short hair as that of a deer or an antelope. His chest area was wide and built. He had speed out of this world, and he knew that I was petrified of him. He tortured me for the next few seconds.

I felt myself growing weaker and fainter by the minute. I didn't want to continue this journey because I could not see how in the world I would survive, let alone win. The spirit of the Lord said, "Open your mouth and sing the words that I tell you to repeat. Order my steps in your Word, dear Lord. Lead me, guide me every day, and send your anointing Father. I pray, order my steps in your Word."

I thought what a strange request, especially at a time I deemed that I was fighting for my life. I asked, "You want me to sing?" One thing for sure, in that particular moment, if I were to survive, I needed the Lord to order and ordain my steps.

After I sung the verse, I was instructed to look back up at the beast, and when I did, I noticed right away that the emotions, fear, doubt, uncertainty, defeat, and doom had all been transferred from me to him, the beast. He was stronger in might, yet he was now trembling in my sight. I could hear him laboring to breathe and struggling just to keep pace with me. I was in awe of what I was now witnessing.

The spirit of the Lord spoke to me and said, "Looking at the beast will become a necessary entity to your journey because oftentimes when you are running from him you must realize he is just as afraid of you, and his desire is to convince you that he is more powerful than your God-given ability and strength.

"When you refuse to look at him, you empower him to believe the lie that he believes, inevitably providing him with false empowerment of your destiny. He only has whatever you relinquish to him. If you demonstrate fear, that is what he will use against you to fight you. If you display doubt, defeat, or any other misgivings, he will use your very thoughts or expressed weakness to steal your joy and your victory. Every now and then, the spirit of God will instruct you to face your enemy!"

What I noticed about myself was that in facing the beast, my footsteps had suddenly slowed down tremendously, and now I ran with assurance, confidence, control, purpose, and guidance. Not only did I feel stronger, I was suddenly energized to stay focused and determined to win. I was instructed by the spirit of God to keep singing. So I continued with, "Humbly I ask you teach me your will while you are working help me to keep still. Satan is busy, God is real. Order my steps in your Word."

By this time, I heard this awful screeching noise—the kind where it is indicated that excruciating pain is associated with it. I looked over at the beast to find him in agonizing pain, limping in fact. He was now running in a disoriented manner, unsure of his gait or direction he should take. He was sweating profusely and gasping for breath. I almost felt sorry for him but suddenly remembered, it was my enemy, the one who came to not only eat of my flesh, but to destroy me without a cause.

Refusing to give up quite so easily, the beast continued to struggle alongside me, moaning and groaning all the way, looking pitiful by the minute and disgusting the rest of the way. I came around the first hurdle the woman mentioned to me earlier when I got a glimpse of that picture in my spirit.

I realized that I was almost there, so I pressed toward the mark even stronger and more confidently. As I crossed over the first bridge, I was instructed to look over at the beast again and say, "The blood of Jesus." I did so with confidence, and the beast screamed as though I had punched him in the face. It was a hollowing scream, and this time, he began to fall backwards as if losing his balance. Reeling, trying to stay abreast, he stared at me to just give up the race. I thought of the story of David and Goliath.

David said to the Philistine, "You come against me with sword and spear and javelin, but I come against you in the name of the Lord Almighty, the God of the armies of Israel, whom you have defied…today I will give the carcasses of the Philistine army to the birds of the air…and the whole world will know that there is a God in Israel… it is not by sword or spear that the Lord saves; for the battle is the Lord's, and he will give all of you into our hands. (1 Sam. 17:45–47, NIV)

I did not possess a spear or an audience to cheer me on. What I did have was the promise of God that he would never leave me or forsake me, and that in the time of trouble, he would hide me. So I decided to press on toward the mark. Gaining progress, my legs were strengthened, my back was straightened, my vision was cleared, my mind was made up, and I knew right then and there that nothing would keep me from seeing and experiencing the true salvation of God.

After crossing the bridge, now came the final hurdle, and it's within my sight. Praise God, praise God was my testimony. With every completed step, I noticed that with lifting up and putting down my feet on new ground, something incredible was taking place in my spirit.

It looked as though my feet were being dipped into fresh concrete that had just been poured on sight, and when I lifted up my feet to move forward, the old footprint became an immediate legacy that would serve as a reminder that my original steps had been ordered and ordained by the Almighty God who is the first and the last, the beginning and the end.

As I was clearly coming to the end of this particular part in the journey, I had just one more hurdle to deal with. As I kept running, I was instructed by the spirit to look down at my arms, and when I did, to my delight, there was something unique dangling from them. As I stretched out my right arm, I kept seeing these letters. At first I could not make out what they meant. Upon closer examination, I discovered what was written in the bones of both my arms—the word victory on both sides.

The words were not only written on both of my arms, but clearly, the Y hung off the tips of my fingers, and they were also embedded on both of my legs, making it virtually impossible to escape the sight, notion, and evidence that I need not fight this fight because Daddy (God) had already been there, done that, and paid the entire bill in full!

Well, I not only crossed over the last hurdle in record time, but I looked over at the beast and said one final goodbye. I said, "In the name of Jesus, I have the victory." With this, I crossed over the last bridge designed to keep animals inside the pasture. The bridge was made in a tic-tac-toe fashion, and anything with hooves would not be able to cross. This meant my enemy would forever be bound and could only come so far even in the now!

This time, he not only staggered but fell completely onto the ground, leaving a tremendous hole filled with black dirt and stench. I crossed over safely and with record speed. Only to be met by a cab driver who was dressed appropriately—in uniform and cap. He got out of the car, smiled at me, and tipped his hat. He drove ever so carefully. He didn't speed, he wasn't in a hurry, and he appeared to be right on schedule. He came around to the passenger door for me and beckon for me to enter.

When I did, I remembered that I did not ask the woman her name and wished that I had done so. I thought to myself, Lord,

I forgot to ask for her name. I wanted to thank her for helping me to get home.

Just then, I heard a voice that sounded like thunder in the distance. When I looked up into the sky, just above the trees, there she was again—the beautiful black woman with immaculate skin not a blemish anywhere and perfect smile and teeth. She was waving at me as if she was cheering me on and that I had passed "this" test.

The woman said, "Bye, Brenda." As she continued to waive, I did likewise and said thank you several times over. Tears were streaming down my face from gratitude. I then turned around and got into the car. The cab driver closed the door, and we drove away, humming a little praise and worship tune together. Little did I know the battle of reality would start right away, and it continues to this day, just in a different manner.

AN UNEXPECTED TURN

After being unemployed for about a month, I applied for various positions through temporary agencies, and to my surprise, I got a job opportunity with an oil and gas company. I enjoyed my relationship with my boss. He was funny, outgoing, and a great dresser. He made lots and lots of money signing humongous oil and gas leases; and when he moved forward in advancements, eventually so did I.

I continued to work for the oil and gas company for the next four and a half years as an oil and gas lease secretary. Rubbing elbows with the best of them and eating out in some of Texas's finest restaurants. It was great exposure while it lasted. One day, my boss and several of the other department managers were in Houston at a conference when the housekeeping lady showed up to empty the trash and clean the offices as usual; however, on this particular day, she asked me if she could speak to me for just a moment. I said yes and felt comfortable with her doing so.

The housekeeping lady closed the door and said that she wanted to pray with me and asked if that was okay. Again, not a big deal, during the prayer, the housekeeping lady held my hand and began to pray in English first and then in Spanish. Afterwards, she said, "Ms. Murphy, the Lord is going to bless you with a heart of ministry and eventually, you will leave your worldly job and do the ministry of the Lord."

Shocked and taken aback, I interrupted the woman and tried to say something when the housekeeping lady said, "No need to worry or fret, the Lord will take care of you."

Even though the housekeeping lady gave me her telephone number and the name of her church, I was never able to speak with her again, nor did I see this woman again. While I was excited about doing ministry, I had to get use to receiving prophecy and where it all fit into my life. I couldn't understand why I couldn't do both work in the secular world and do ministry as well.

After all, God knew that I needed a job, so why would he take away my earthly livelihood to give me a "heart of ministry" when it appeared that I could just as easily done both? For sure, I tried to block that completely out of my head altogether. However, the more I tried, the more the reality was settling in. I started to pray and fast, as well as read my Bible more and more, looking for answers.

After all, I really loved my job. By now, I was making more money than I had ever made in my entire life. I thought this was really not a good time for me to leave my employment and besides, I was already very active in my church. Really, I was.

In January 1996, it seemed like the wind was let out of my sails as it relates to my job. I woke up one morning, and I didn't want to go to work anymore. I really didn't have a valid reason for the feeling I just didn't want to go. I thought I was really losing my mind.

I cried, prayed, fasted, cried some more, and then told Audie I didn't want to go back to work even when just the week before, I absolutely loved my job. For the next several weeks, I vowed to fake it until I could make sense out of what was going on.

Finally, I got in touch with the lady who had previously prayed for me, and we talked for a few minutes, but what I noticed was while I was trying to talk about the prophecy, the lady couldn't recall everything she had said. In fact, she said to me, "That word wasn't for me to remember. It was for you.

I do not have any recollection of what God is doing in your life or any of the specifics. You should seek God for yourself, and he will guide and direct you." Talk about being alone on the isle of Patmos. I felt as though I had been vacationing there for several weeks. After weeks of faking it until I could make sense of it all, my boss came into my office and closed the door. "Brenda, what's wrong?" he asked. I said nothing. "I am fine," with the brightest smile I could muster.

"Why on earth would you ask?" My heart was beating so fast I had to check it once or twice just to make sure it was still in my chest. We talked for about five minutes when my boss finally said, "I know that you are no longer happy here. I can see it on your face. Is there something that we can do for you? Would you be happy with more money, a bigger office, and more vacation time off?"

I thought to myself, you had me at more money. However, as crazy as this may sound, I knew in my heart that I was not in control of anything. I could feel this door closing behind me, and the next chapter of my life was getting ready to begin. Two weeks later, I gave my resignation letter.

My boss asked me why. All I could say, with tears rolling down my face, was it was due to ministry and that God had a call on my life that resonated so profoundly in my heart. I could not stop it or turn it around if I tried. He asked me how I was going to make it financially. I was honest and told him I didn't know. I hadn't had to cross that bridge yet, but I believed that once I got to it, the Lord would provide.

My boss told me, with tears in his eyes, that he didn't understand it, but that he wanted the very best for me and wrote me a personal check that day for an entire month of salary in addition to a severance package. God showed me favor despite my personal uncertainties, not about him but about where I was supposed to be going or doing at that particular time my life.

During the first several weeks of being unemployed, it was like a long beautiful vacation for me. Then I remembered I wasn't getting a paycheck at the end of the rainbow. I remembered every paycheck period, and I did this for a long time. One day, during my routine walks, I was meditating on the fact that I would not be receiving my bi-weekly paycheck and started questioning whether or not I should have left in the first place.

At that very moment, the Spirit of the Lord said, "Don't just remember the good old days, but remember it all including the days of typing major oil and gas leases with tight deadlines, endless meetings, and countless reports and on and on." All of a sudden, I remembered that all was well after all.

At church on Sunday, I was asked to do a few words of encouragement before the pastor spoke. I shared with the congregation my decision to leave work and go after what I felt God was calling me to do. I did not do it for the applause of mankind or the solicitation of those who volunteered to readily give me their expert advice on the subject matter.

Nevertheless, I decided to move forward despite opposition and my personal doubts and fears. Besides, it was too late. I was already treading water, and there was no turning back. I believed God would provide all that I needed for that day's journey. The next day, while leaving intercessory prayer, the pastor approached me and asked, "Did you really quit your job? What did your husband say? If the Lord told you, then you must obey him and that he was fine with my decision." The pastor looked at me as though I had lost my everlasting mind.

Then he went on to say, "What are you going to do?" I said, "Trusting God and moving forward. What else is there to do?" He shook his head and walked away. I believe that he did so because at the time, perhaps God may have been challenging him to do the same as it relates to full-time ministering.

As time progressed, the Lord began to open up many doors of speaking engagements and opportunities to do ministry both in and out of church settings for me. There were many times I was asked to teach weekly bible sessions for various churches, women groups, Bible studies, retreats, and etc.

One particular event I was asked to go to in Oklahoma City, to speak to a singles group. However upon arrival, the only person who was warm, kind, and inviting was the lady who invited me. In fact, the mistress of ceremony was rude to the core and didn't mind showing it.

The chairperson said to me the very first time she met me, "In Oklahoma, we expect nothing but the best." Later it would be revealed to me that the woman had originally taken my resume and threw it in the garbage because it was not impressive enough for her and therefore she deemed me not being sophisticated enough to be on the program.

So I decided to keep from being rude to her, I asked if I may speak in the moment, and the woman's reply to me was yes. My words were: "First of all, you are short, so I will take off my shoes so that I can be almost your height. Therefore, I will not have to speak over your head. Secondly, I do not perform for anyone.

To the very best of my ability, I don't ever remember performing in the circus, and I will not be taking my assignments today. I have come to do the will of who has sent me and nothing else." God not only allowed me to be received that day, but I was invited back to that same church three more times.

After a short period of me being unemployed, the Lord sent me out on another assignment. This time, it was to work for the distinguished furniture corporation. I absolutely loved their furniture and all of their accessories, so I was excited to work for them. During the interview process, I met with a woman named Nancy, and she appeared to be so sweet and professional, even inviting. She talked to me about the customer service position that she had available.

During our conversation, she said to me, "I have the perfect fit for you here at our corporate office. We have had a supervisory position that has been available for several months now, and I think you would be perfect for it." The red flag went up when she said "available for months." Really, in this economy? I thought.

For some reason, I was not interested in the supervisory position and told her so during the interview. Days after the interview, she continued calling me at least three different times and asked me out to lunch. I thanked her for the calls, but once again, informed her that I was not interested in the position. There was just something about this woman's demeanor, personality, fake smile, and everything that did not set well with me. It had to do with more or less what she was not saying that scared me the most.

Days and even weeks later, she continued to call and relentlessly tried to entice me into taking the position. After praying and asking the Lord for direction on this matter, I felt the Holy Spirit leading me to take it. Quite frankly, I would have rather worked on a farm all day in a hundred degree weather first without a mule than to take this position, especially under her leadership. I did not have a good feeling about her then or afterwards. It was only after I took the position did I realize my instincts were correct.

When I called the manager back, I continued praying the whole time that I was speaking with her and told her that I had a change of heart and that I would accept the position after all. She screamed and was too thrilled to hear the news. For me, however, I hung up the phone and cried myself to sleep. This one I thought was going to cost me dearly. By now, one thing that I was definitely familiar with was demonic activity. I could sense their presence and their demeanor quite well, and their eyes never lie no matter what.

On Monday morning, I showed up for work bright eyed and bushy tailed, regretting it all the way. Nancy and her secretary,

Theresa, were at the door and greeted me with great big smiles and hugs. Once again, they took me out to lunch. Over the next couple of days, I met the team that I would be supervising, and I couldn't tell if I had been privileged to the funeral before the benediction, or had I made it too late after the bodies had been disposed of because 90 percent of the people I met during orientation was already gone—at least spiritually speaking—and the other 10 percent appeared that it was just a matter of time.

One of the many tasks was to setup a call center atmosphere where the customer service representatives would be able to have ongoing customer service training once a month. They would be able to have their calls monitored and feedback given to them weekly. Their calls would be assessed so that they would know what their expectations were and if they were meeting their required goals or not.

I was shocked that after meeting and talking with each of the representatives, they had never been given this opportunity by Nancy or her assistant to improve. When I probed more about why not, each of them said that for starters, Ms. Nancy don't like people. She doesn't come out of her office except to scream at people and make threats about their job security.

After hearing this over and over again from several representatives, I got my purse, lifted up the church finger, and commenced to walk first then started running to my car. Not only did I get in my car and leave the premises, but I also burned rubber on the way out. Needless to say, after a couple of days, Nancy called me and asked what happened. I wanted to say that the more appropriate question would have been what didn't.

She tried to appear shocked, but I would later learn that this was her usual MO. She didn't want anyone telling her anything. She would go as far as to say that she is the one who called the shots around there and what she says goes. Not only was this woman a true nutcase that was let out of the psych ward much too soon, she did not like taking pictures of herself at all.

This became evident on one of our many "team building out-ings." It was right before Christmas, and the group and I had all went out to celebrate survival week of mad inventory of the stores and warehouses, which was what it really should have been called. In the spirit of Christmas, everyone put on a brave front and called it an office celebration. Well, there is grace for every-thing, including this psycho.

Someone brought along their camera and unbeknown to Nancy, they snapped her picture while everyone was together eat-ing. One picture in particular was one by herself, and the other picture represented the group. Man oh man, that woman came unglued, girdle, and all. She went totally off her rocker on the poor unsuspecting representatives, screaming, ranting, grabbing her hair, turning bright red and yelling, "I don't do pictures, I don't do pictures give it to me, give it to me!" It was like watching Chucky 3 in 3D while the children were singing "Oh Christmas Tree."

After sixteen long incredible months of life in "Egypt," I did give her notice that I was leaving because I was in a win-less situation. Nancy was extremely domineering and controlling. She wanted to talk to people any kind of way and dared others to defend themselves. During the time before I gave her notice, a caller had complained about items that had been sold out over the holidays, and there were not any left in the store room.

All the stores and all the warehouses were completely sold out. When I informed the customer of that, the customer became belligerent and cursed me completely out but not before saying, "What's your name? I want you to know that I could buy you,"

To which I responded, "Now that's where you are absolutely wrong. I am not for sale, rent, lease, loan, or layaway now or ever. Now, is there anything else I may be able to assist you with today?"

The customer hung up and called and spoke with Nancy who had been locked up in her office all week, refusing to come out to even speak to her employees or even say good night on her way out the door. This was a woman that never offered encouragement to anyone else but would not hesitate to write an employee up or to fire them at the drop of a hat, and yet she was considered as a customer service director.

Nancy was livid. Once I was inside Nancy's office, Nancy began yelling, screaming, and pointing her finger directly into my face, shouting, "You'd better be careful how you talk with my customers, or I will throw you out of my office. Do you understand me?" Getting over the shock, I looked over at both Nancy and her boss as she continued to openly berate me in front of him, and of course, he said nothing at all. Finally coming up for air, she said, "Well, do you have anything to say?"

I said, "Oh, I'm sorry were you talking to me just a few minutes ago. I wasn't saying anything because it appeared as though you may have been addressing a little child, and I didn't respond because I am not one. I am assured that you wouldn't be talking to me like that." She became more enraged, stating she can talk to me any way she pleased because she was my boss.

I said to the both of them, "It's been interesting during my tenure here. However, there is absolutely no way am I going to allow anyone to talk to me in the tone of voice and disrespect as you have just attempted to do. I continued to say, "When the customer called and asked about that particular item, I informed her as I had many other customers, that we no longer had that item in stock and that it was an item that was only sold during the holiday season.

Once they were gone, they were all gone. The customer became noticeably enraged and immediately went into a barrage of insults, to which she concluded she could buy me. With that, I didn't need an executive board to make a decision about me, I was done. No one makes me over, and no one will attempt to reduce me to zero and think that I am going to respect, honor, or bow down to them no matter color, creed, ignorance, or stupidity. Now do you hear me? Or perhaps I should ask you, do you understand?"

At that moment, her boss said to me that was not the way he heard about it from Nancy who told him a different story. He apologized on behalf of the customer. Being called into the unscheduled meeting, he asked Nancy to not only apologize but that I should be given a raise. Of course, neither ever happened. It didn't matter. I quit any way.

Nancy refused to pay me for any work done, and even scheduled herself to be out on vacation for the next two weeks. What was meant for evil, God did indeed turn it around for my good. Not only was I paid for two weeks, but I was also paid for unused vacation time, holiday pay, and sick leave.

I was also given a bonus at the same time! All the while, Nancy was out of the office trying to make sure that I would not get paid at all before I left the company. I was also told by the company's executives that if I wanted to come back and work there again, I could. I honestly didn't think so. However, it was nice of them to offer.

HIGHER LEVEL, BIGGER DEVILS

After leaving the distinguished furniture corporate office, I interviewed for a position with a call center as a call center manager. I ended up getting the job and managed a team of twelve call center representatives. Those were the days. From their humble beginnings, my team eventually grew to twenty-five and then to thirty-five back down to twelve.

I managed the customer service department first. Then was promoted to balance transfer department. Afterward I transferred to the acquisitions department, where I managed the managers for short stints of time. While the experience was great, my nerves were shot in the process, but God!

The interesting thing about working for this company, no two days or hours were ever alack. Both customer service off and on the phone were a riot. That entire experience was definitely as my current boss would say, "It ain't for the faint hearted." The joys of being cursed out at 5:00 a.m., threatened to have your tires slashed before noon if you didn't lower the customer's annual percentage rates (APRs), to representatives calling out the day before telling you that they were going to be sick on Tuesday, even when the day just begun on Monday. I mean who wouldn't miss all that love?

For the next eight years, boy oh boy did I ever learn how to grow up quickly. Every waking moment was nothing less than a challenge. For that matter, just getting across the parking lot safely with my purse in hand or intact was a blessing in disguise.

Some days, I wondered if I was going to get car jacked on my way inside the building or on my way to the car.

People drove so incredibly fast across the parking lot, you never knew if you were going to get sideswiped or just simply ran over because very few obeyed speed bumps or human bumps for that matter.

One Saturday morning, while monitoring my team taking calls, I witnessed some strange activity on a different team, so I decided to chime in by listening from remote monitoring to see what was happening. Two ladies were plotting about how to conger up a lie to tell me about a supposed emergency that would be coming around the mountain in a couple of minutes. The plot was one of the ladies would make up the lie while the other would pretend that the lie was about herself and her "dying" grandmother who lived in Louisiana.

This is too cute and sad all at the same time. The two ladies are oblivious about the fact that their calls could be monitored by a manager at any time during their shifts. In fact, I could tell they were quite comfortable in their scheming. So miss ring leader approached me, all dressed up in her party clothes and five layers of makeup, and said as only a true Texan can say, "Skruz me, I need to talk to you…you see an emergency has arisen, and we must leave now to go to Louisiana."

Acting totally surprised and worried all at the, same time, I said, "Oh my goodness, what's wrong?" The ring leader points to the other would be actress and said, "See, her grandmother is dying, and we were told that we needed to get to Louisiana as fast as we could." Catching my breath in the moment of it all, I stood up from behind my desk, looked the ladies straight in their eyes and said, "And do what when you arrive there?"

One of the ladies replied, "Well, see her grandmother is like a real grandmother to me so I must go too for moral support." By now, the gig was up, so I said, "Okay, but the two of you must understand that I cannot advise you one way or the other, however, I will send an e-mail to both of your supervisors to keep them in the loop that you both left early." I believe that I saw some of their makeup dry up right before my eyes.

Appearing to be shocked by this response, they both went and sat down at their desks never to return again. I absolutely loved it! During my tenure at the call center, life really could change in a twinkling of an eye. Moment by moment, something interesting always happened, one had to be more than ready for it. By year two, I had already had more than five different senior managers to my credit. Some helpful and others, well, thank God they didn't last long.

Even though the job was so very stressful, I enjoyed my work because I absolutely loved making a difference in the lives of my coworkers, enemies, and my customers. Through it all, I grew from all my experiences as my coworkers and my bosses certainly got the blood out of a Muppet from my labor in the process of it all. I wasn't quite sure what I was going to do after I left the call center, but somehow I knew life would keep getting interesting for me.

In March of 2003, my dad passed away. Before the death of my dad, I had a vision one night of my father's death; the entire celebration of his homecoming was remarkable. The vision started out with this huge body of clear, calm water, and on it sat at least four to five beautiful yachts seemingly with every amenity known to mankind.

The guests were all adorned with after-five evening wear (black and white penguin attire I called it). All the people on board were laughing and appearing to be having a grand time. While I was not privileged to the party, I could see from a distance as though a spectator everything that was going on. During this celebration, there was a real sense of true peace and genuine happiness had by all who attended.

Directly across the street was the old church where all of my family members grew up, including my parents and their parents. It appeared to be around 6:00 a.m. to 8:00 a.m. because the cold, fresh dew was still very present on the grass. There were lots of cars parked on the grounds of this little old wooden familiar church, and people were lined for hours around the building, waiting to get in to get a seat.

I remembered asking those individuals that I was familiar with what's going on. What the gathering was about. And someone finally turned around to me and said, "You don't know? It's a celebration."

Just as I was going to inquire even further, I looked to my right and saw a little house that is still standing today behind the little church. Across this pasture, people were going in and out of it, and it caught my attention. So I decided to go over and check it out. After entering the house, I realized that I should not have come uninvited, so I held the door knob as I tried to enter in a conspicuous way and hoped that no one would notice.

However, just as I was closing the door back, I turned around, and there was this beautiful woman who sat upon a stool, stirring something in this rather large pot. The woman's skin appeared to be absolutely radiant. Not a blemish, pimple, or anything. She was perfect. She had this glow about herself that was absolutely priceless. I could not put my finger on it, but it was mind boggling.

I looked down suddenly at the flooring and saw that the floor itself was glistening, almost like a special type of formula had been placed on it. It was crystal clear and had no blemishes. The walls were like that of a museum. The jewels and gems it displayed were as though each piece came out of the wall to be looked upon at the right timing. Further down the hall was this gentleman dressed up in this vintage suit, looking at what appeared to be artwork on the wall. He had a top hat on and a pipe in his mouth. His countenance appeared to be that of a Scottish man.

After being there probably longer than I should, I decided it was time for me to go and I made my grand exit in silence. Just as I put my hand on the door knob, I asked God what was that look that the woman had on her person, and this was the reply that I was given by the Holy Spirit: "That's my peace upon her." Until that time, I had never in my life experienced or seen such a look before. I didn't think that I ever would again on this side of heaven. As I exited the house, the woman said to me, "Now you are coming to the party, aren't you, Brenda?" I was surprise that she even noticed me, let alone knew my name. Stammering, Brenda said, "Yes, I guess."

I remembered thinking to myself, wow there was absolutely no sadness at all about this moment. Nothing but joy was displaced in the vision. I could tell only peace and happiness was there. During the vision, before I woke up, I remembered feeling my heart being shattered and me crying out to God no not now, please not now. At that moment, I felt as though someone took my heart, broke it into two pieces, and gave me one half; heaven kept the other. I remembered waking up screaming and lying on the floor in pure pain, spiritually.

Exactly three weeks later, Audie called me at work to tell me the news that Pops, my dad, had gone home to be with the Lord. My heart broke for my mother. To hear her crying got the very best of me. I hurt for my mother. I missed my dad so much, and it had only been a couple of days. God, please give our family the strength we needed to move forward. On the drive home for the funeral, I reminisced about times with my dad, and of course the tears came in waves.

I leaned on God even the more. While at home making the preparation for Dad's funeral with my siblings, it was extremely difficult to do so. We all hurt and missed our dad tremendously; his jokes, his story telling, and his laughter. He was the super glue for our family. This loss was going to be felt throughout our family for years to come. My dad passed away on Friday, one week before my birthday on March 26.

On that Sunday, my oldest sister and I visited my old friend Pastor Mardell's church in Mississippi once again. The service was wonderful, and at the end, he called us up to the front of the church and gave us both a word from the Lord. To my sister, he said something along the lines that our family will make it through this moment and that God would see us through. He encouraged us to hang in there and keep the faith.

Then, the pastor suddenly turned to me and began to laugh hysterically. Quite frankly, I didn't seem amused and wondered why or what he thought was so funny, but I didn't question his motives either. As I stood there, looking at him, the laughter didn't appear to be vicious or vindictive or out of a sense of rudeness, but more or less like, "C'mon, really?" As me and my sister stood at the altar, the pastor continued to laughed as we looked at him. He finally stopped and said directly to me, "Now, daughter, you know if you were born a man, you would have been tired of having your own church?"

He was staring right into my eyes. I felt so sheepish. Because I had recently made that very same comment under my breath to Audie, and now here he was exposing me right before his congregation. What he may not have known that there weren't a lot of people male and female too keen on the idea of me walking in my purpose then or ever. Well, before I admitted to anyone, including myself, about walking in my purpose, to some degree, I wanted to escape the entire negative backlash I was sure to come once I did.

I knew all too well that there would be some individuals who would throw me up under the bus, sell me out, walk out, and even doubt my call from God. Some would only be too happy to bring up what they believe was my past and too eager to pronounce doom and gloom on my future. I didn't fear man, but I wanted to be placed somewhere to preach the gospel to those who really understood the need for God's presence in their lives who didn't feel that they had already arrived.

Anyway, Pastor Mardell continued with, "You and your husband will have a ministry together." You will have your own church. By then, I was saying under my breath, while looking at him, "Um, it will probably be somewhere down in the boom docks because I know it won't be in Texas." I was not being smart mouth about it, but I knew all too well the ungodly reaction and backbiting I was already receiving from a lot of the so-called saints, even as I served in the church faithfully. Even in that, most folks still deemed that as being "harmless" as long as I didn't mention the preached word.

The thought of individuals who would rather hear me deny my call altogether rather than preach the gospel whereby people could be saved was mind boggling, especially when they so readily proclaimed to be Christians themselves. Nevertheless, by the time I finished the last word of my thought process, Pastor Mardell was getting ready to walk away.

Then he suddenly turned around and said, "And it won't be in the middle of nowhere either; the only reason why you do not have your own church is because He has to get some of the people ready for you and ready to receive you. It's not about you being ready. God has to prepare their hearts to receive you."

I wanted to cry right there at the altar, not out of a sense of joyfulness but out of a sense of humbleness and a sense of desperately needing extra grace and God's protection for my life and daily direction. Many people saw me daily, and assumed that all was well, when deep inside I was hurting from those who pretended to be my friend. There were those who took daily pleasure in my woundedness, who were lying and scandalizing my name, gossiping about things they didn't have any true knowledge about.

At times, there were church members who I went to the various hospitals, homes, and in specific locations and laid hands on and prayed for their loved ones and witnessed God heal and raised up now put their mouth on me out of a sense of dislike because they didn't think that a woman should or could preach the gospel. Many walked away, looked the other way, and simply sold me out for their own personal name sake and devotion to what others may say or think of them.

Not only was I made fun of because of my walk and love of Christ and what He had fashioned my purpose to be, but from time to time, there were those in leadership roles who felt the need to provide me with their specific opinions about my call as well. At times going as far as to verbally express who and to whom God could use and would use. I was called names such as "holy roller," and even mocked for wearing my clothes a certain length at times.

For me personally, many of Sundays when these antics were being expressed, it was painful to notice how many Judas betrayed me on one given day. Many of whom felt free to call upon me when there was trouble in their homes, marriages, finances, children, and grandchildren's lives.

There were many men and women, whose marriages were on the rocks and considered it to be over, and yet they sought my wisdom at interval times and asked me to pray and fast with them only to be delivered by God yet they found it effortless to then sell me out for a little bit of nothing.

When I tell you that God kept me in the midst of it all, it would be an understatement. God not only kept me, but he covered my goings and comings in His blood, and He alone made me whole. Thank you precious Jesus! After receiving that word from the Lord at Pastor Mardell's church, the next few days of getting prepared for my dad's funeral made it even more taxing and thought provoking for me.

The day came when I had to get ready for my dad's funeral, and I purposely tried to avoid riding in the family car. I just didn't want to go through that phase of it because it made everything so surreal and final for me. Frances's request prevailed as she specifically asked me to ride with her and others in the family car. That was one of the longest rides for me.

I had hoped that I would never have to take. By the time we had reached the church, the vision I had of my father's death definitely ranged true. As I looked around at the scenery, it felt like I was stepping into the very vision I had recently had about my dad's death. I just silently prayed. "Lord, God please keep us strong in this hour for we need you now more than ever."

As the family entered the church grounds, I noticed this particular jeep, a Tracker I think it's called, and out of it came these three men—the pastor, his assistant, and another minister. I was shocked and floored to see them because they had actually driven all the way from Texas to Mississippi, spending the night in Jackson and driving the next day to Macon to attend my father's funeral with me. That particular moment was priceless to me and will never be forgotten.

Paying my last respects to the viewing of the body of my father was numbing at best. Seeing his body in the casket became crystal clear to me that he did not live there on earth anymore and that he was safely home with his Lord. As the services began, my pastor from Texas prayed for me and blessed my family. It meant the world to me for his presence being there and praying for our family.

The service was warm and inviting; it was moving to say the least. However, right before the end of the sermon, I simply got up and walked out of the church. I needed fresh air. I thought that I was alone but soon found out that I wasn't. I was actually surrounded by my niece, my pastor, and the other ministers. In that moment, there are no words that could be said to comfort another because my heart was truly broken and a piece of me was missing as well.

I remembered it vividly. As I stood under that beautiful shade tree, I prayed and asked God, "Lord, I know that you do not owe me anything, but if it is your will, please let me know if dad made it home." In that same instance, I was privileged to a vision in which I saw what looks to be a huge industrial building likened to a hospital, where the exit was on the back of the building. I saw my dad running down the stairs on his way out of this building. He never looked back as he neared the bottom of the staircase. There were two big doors that clearly reflected one way out. There would be no reentering in through the same doors that were used for exit.

Once my dad reached those doors and placed his hands on the handles, he pushed slightly, and the doors flung open. The brightest and soothing light that I ever witnessed illuminated from the sky. It was breathtaking. At that moment, I recognized that my dad had begun to run and never, ever stopped. The bright lights seemed to engulf him, and then the doors closed shut behind him.

When I asked God about what I saw, this is what was spoken in my heart by the Holy Spirit: "The exit was likened to a wrought iron hanger where one may put silk material on it, and it slides right off of it because the garment is unable to grasp a hold and remain to the hanger. While your father was going down the stairs, he was considered still in this life (the earthly realm), but the minute his hands laid hold of those handles, and he pushed through to the other side, (the heavenly realm), nothing on this side of life can no longer harm, hurt, or hinder him. Nothing no one can say, do, or bring up against him, will matter any longer." I recognized in that moment, my father was now indeed home finally at rest.

While I was standing at the grave site, everyone was returning to their cars. I thought I was alone, so I stood there, talking to my dad when I heard the leaves rustling. I turned to see what or who it was, and it was actually my pastor standing by my side to give me words of encouragement. I was appreciative and very thankful that he was there by my side during this very important and pivotal time in my life and the life of my family.

The next several days, weeks, and months were quite critical for my family and me. Each day was taken through prayer one minute at a time. My heart ached for my brother Eddie, because in my opinion, he endured the most pain and woundedness by being at home with our dad and taking him to various doctor appointments. In the end, our dad had secretly sworn Eddie to secrecy and asked him to take care of his mom after he was gone.

I could not even imagine what that was like. It must have been one of the hardest things that he had ever done. As he cried, I held him in my arms and told him it is going to be alright. To hear my brother say, "Faye, I did all that I could do. Dad told me to take care of mom. I did all that I could do." I felt his personal pain, and I was never more proud of him than in that particular moment.

In my opinion, Eddie never truly got a fighting chance because unfortunately there are those individuals who lay in wait to devour, destroy, and discredit another individual's name and reputation at any available opportunity that they can. Their words can be ruthless, cold, calculated, demeaning, deliberately setting out to harm and sabotage another's life right from the beginning without so much as batting an eye or possessing an ounce of remorse in the process. Not only does the enemy lie and do each of God's children a disservice, they scout for other recruits who are more than willing to join the group to further discredit that individual's integrity.

Often what is interesting to me is when that pain of a lie, gossip, test, or trial is brought up in questioning by the individual who has been wronged, the individual who started it all has the audacity to be offended, hurt, wounded; and nine times out of ten can be counted on to look and appear to be the "victim." They often pretend, sometime sheepishly as if they have no earthly idea how the rumor or lie ever came about. Really?

The problem with our society today is that it is quite comfortable continuing with the lack of respect for privacy, honesty, and blatant disregard of another person's well-being. As a people, society is very quick to judge. We are definitely, in most cases, the accuser of the brethren without a cause; and at times, are quite frankly darn proud of it. The world has no problem with raining on the other's parade. Selling the other out, spying on and making it their personal business to tell someone else's business; cutting the other down without thought or resolve; and quick to ask God, "Why am I having so much trouble in my life all in the same breath.

Often afterward, the question is sometimes asked, "Why am I having it so hard? I am a good person, I go to church regularly. I pay my tithes, I sing in the choir, I feed the community, and so forth and so on."

Nevertheless, about a month after our dad passing, his spirit came to visit me at our home. The vision was a duplicate of that previous year's family Thanksgiving together. It was a joyous time well spent with siblings, family, and friends. I could not have asked for a better, more meaningful time spent together. In fact, I had spent that prior year praying to God and asking him to allow my family and me to spend one more holiday together. Little did I know that would be the very last time I would spend that time with my dad. God was indeed gracious to me and my family.

In the vision, my family was all gathered together eating, laughing, talking, and having a grand old time when I heard this soft but very familiar voice above all the noise call my name. It was the way my dad would call me. In that instance, I knew that it was my dad's voice, no doubt about it.

He had on an outfit I knew all too well. Plaid shirt, khaki pants, and black shoes—he was even wearing his little glasses on the end of his nose. He was smiling a big bright smile, and his arms were outstretched to hug me. He called my name, and I called his, leaping into his arms. We were just holding each other.

Suddenly, I remembered that he was no longer on the earth with the family anymore and when I said, "But, you're…" He immediately pulled back and placed his finger up to his lips and shushed me. With that, all I could do was watch my dad disappear from my sight. It was wonderful to see him again. I missed him terribly, but I knew in my heart I would see him again soon. From time to time I often heard my father's voice through songs in my spirit. My father thoroughly enjoyed singing hymnals in fact; they were his favorite songs to sing.

When I would hear his voice in my spirit singing, I would immediately chime in as well. I would safely say that from time to time, I felt my dad's presence around for about a month after he had passed away, and it really felt great to be near him. I wasn't afraid of him; it just felt natural that he would linger. I would often ask my mom if she ever sensed his presence around her and she would say, no, can't say for sure. Somehow I had a feeling he was around. She may have just missed the obvious.

In July of 2003, Audie and I went home to a wedding. While we were there visiting, Audie was admitted to the hospital. He had had a heart attack in the same room where my dad had passed away just a few short months earlier. My dad passed in March 2003, and Audie's heart attack happened in July of 2003. Thank God my brother Eddie was home and found him on the floor, calling out for help. It was nothing but grace and mercy that caused Eddie who was outside on the porch, to hear my husband calling for help.

Audie told me that when he was calling for help, he could feel himself getting out of breath and thought that he would try calling out for help one last time. He said with all his might, he used everything within himself to say help, and by that time, the door opened and there came Eddie who picked him up and was carrying him outside when help showed up to take Audie to the emergency room. Mom and I were just returning from the grocery store. I switched vehicles and sat in the back seat of my niece's truck and placed my arms around the front of Audie's seat, begging him to hold on and not to leave me.

I remembered him looking up at me and saying, "Baby, I can't breathe" and passed out. When we arrived at the hospital, everyone got out and went through the emergency room where they took Audie immediately and began to give him oxygen. They wouldn't allow me to see him for quite some time.

I prayed so hard that he would be fine. When it seemed like hours had passed, the hospital finally allowed me to see him. He had oxygen on and was sedated to rest. The doctors were still running tests and did not want to speculate at the moment what the problem might have been. In the meantime, I was content with talking with the doctor, Jesus Christ, and believing that everything was going to be alright.

About four hours had gone past when Audie was finally admitted to a room. I was told indeed he did have a heart attack and that thankfully someone found him and got him to the hospital in the nick of time. God is so good! Unfortunately, the hospital where Audie was not equipped to take care of him for the condition that he was in, and they informed me that they would probably be moving him shortly once they got clearance. True to form, he was moved around 8:00 p.m. to Columbus, Mississippi by ambulance. I rode with him and continued to pray and plead the blood of Jesus over him.

As I prayed, I could feel God's expressed assurance that everything was going to be alright even in the midst of it all. Once we arrived at the next hospital, I was told that it was a great hospital and that it specialized in dealing with patients who experienced having heart attacks only. Audie was immediately placed on a specific floor that dealt with his condition only. I was both thankful and relieved. Finally around 10:30 p.m., a nurse came in and asked me who I was and informed me that Audie would be in for a little fight, but that he would be okay.

I felt others who really cared about us and our family was praying for us as well. The nurse said that Audie had indeed had a heart attack and that the timeframe to get him to the emergency room played a pivotal role in not only saving his life but also in his recovery time to get well. Audie remained in the hospital for another several days before he was released and our drive back home. I continued to pray and seek God's favor because I knew it would be impossible without the Lord's guidance.

On the way back to Texas, I drove. I requested FMLA from my job because I knew that I would need that time off to take care of Audie and to rest myself. Our church family was extremely supportive during this timeframe. Still the workload was enormous, but God was an ever-present help while we were in trouble. Audie's boss, Mona, was nothing short of an angel in disguise. Both Audie and I thanked God for Mona showing us favor and much love. Through Mona's compassion, Audie didn't miss a beat and was able to return to work with vacation and a bonus in tow. God was very faithful!

ACCEPTING MY CALL INTO MINISTRY

"In all your ways acknowledge him,
and he will make your path straight."

—Proverbs 3:6

For a while, things went back to normal and were someone quite in our lives. I was still working for the call center at the time and active in the church. After six months, I was then eligible for a six weeks sabbatical, and boy was I looking forward to spending that time alone and getting some much needed rest and relaxation.

To my surprise, during my first week of sabbatical, God gave me a vision that I was to start a website and a ministry. Within several weeks, the website was up and running with the help and support of a good friend and her husband. The name Innovative Ministries, Inc. was given to me to use. Its purpose is to revive, restore, and renew God's people.

It is a season of change and with change comes transition. The Lord said, "I am taking that which had already been formed and transforming it into something anew." In other words, those individuals who may feel that their lives, dreams, marriages, or chance at something new and refreshing can still happen. My happiness, joy, peace, hope, careers, friendships, or what have you is not over—it can still be restored and used for the master's use.

I immediately called up a friend and shared that what God had given me. She invited me over for lunch, and we talked about the ministry. Later that same day, we came up with the mission and vision statement for the ministry. I made arrangements for our pictures to be taken professionally and my friend's husband agreed to build the website for us.

Later another friend critiqued it, and we were able to go live within a couple of weeks. I was super excited about everything. I shared the information with an individual who I thought was my friend, and said, "Did you see my website link that I sent to you about my ministry?"

The individual said "What website?" I replied, "Mine, Innovative Ministries, Inc." They said, "Oh, that little website? That's yours? I thought it belonged to someone else, and your picture was just a part of it." With that, the individual simply turned and walked away.

I asked God to keep my tears from falling while I was there in the presence of so many. However, as I made it my business to exit the building that night with my dignity still intact, I knew that I would overcome that insult as well. On my way home that night, I simply prayed, "God I know your voice, and this was not it.

Help me to move forward regardless of the pain and rejection that is coming my way." I continued to pray, "Lord, your will and your will only." From that day came more rejection, lies, bitterness, and rumors that I was somehow trying to take over the church or start one for myself.

None of that was remotely true. God had not spoken it, and neither had I asked for it. Yet the root of hatred and malice was already brewing in the hearts, minds, souls, and consciousness of many. They smiled in my face but so readily stabbed me in my back, and not necessarily while it were fully turned away.

God continued to keep me, promote me, and encouraged me. And I never stopped praising, loving, and needing him even the more. In fact, I needed him more and more in my personal journey. The time finally came when I realized that I had to make an executive decision to move forward despite the pain, degradation, hypocrisy, and heartache. God was growing me, and sometimes growing pains are often painful and challenging at best. But with God as the forerunner, all things are indeed possible.

In March of 2005, I began planning my first Women of Purpose Conference and looking for a location to do so. I was lead to call this venue on the other side of Dallas and spoke with a woman named Teresa, who later became my planner for the event. During the planning stages, there were approximately ten women selected to help out in the early planning stages.

Looking back on the whole thing, three of those ten individuals probably really were for me, and the other seven were not. Still God prevailed, and He got all of the glory and the victory of it all. The first conference event was very successful. There were over 275 women in attendance. The women were treated to two nights and three days of conference with a cruise across the lake on a yacht. However due to the weather, we had to cancel; otherwise, the event was received really well.

The enemy tried to work through those who were all too eager to allow him to do so, but there was no defeat. God was yet glorified, and I believed that there were those women who attended who were delivered as well. After the conference, I received enormous motivating feedback from ladies who understood more clearly their purpose and reasoning for being a part of God's great plan for their lives.

From there, I continued to encourage, motivate, coach, and mentor others as God would have me. I would often be appreciated and at other times shunned. I would always notice that whenever I would talk to God about certain things concerning my walk with him, He would say, "Daughter, you have to be made." While I didn't always understand immediately what that meant, I was slowly catching on. In other words, the journey wasn't going to be easy. To put it another way, as my friend Cynthia would say, "It ain't for the faint hearted."

After the first event in March, which was considered the spring event, there were three more planned for the first year. All three were different but successful. Each event was planned with the women in mind. My hope and desire was that through the conference, the women would truly dig deeper into their purpose and make a decision to walk it out in the exact order to how God had planned it for their lives.

During the next seven years of planning, hosting, and leading women conferences, I had never felt more spiritually fulfilled and closer to my personal purpose on earth. Even though I thought one of the best ways to avoid church persecution was to avoid having my event on church property where there was even the slightest possibility of someone thinking that I was planning a major take over.

Well, I was wrong again. The spies went back and put their own personal version on what they deemed I was doing. Some believed that I had a personal motive(s) behind the whole thing that opened up a new can of worms, which didn't take or require much effort to do.

Feeling the pressure and the cool breeze from some of the members of the church, I thought if I stayed under the radar low enough as well as keep my thoughts and purpose to myself, it would be more acceptable by all. Well, that dog wouldn't hunt either and yet again, I found myself once again in the hot seat. Finally, the strain of opposition, the constant attacks on my character, the mindless games that were being played out in both public and private can and at some point took its toll on me.

I became so tired of not knowing which direction the lies and deceit were coming from or concerning myself with which smile really was genuine. So I decided I had had enough of the heartaches, backstabbing, deceit, and disrespect to last a lifetime. It was simply time to let that toxic aspect of my life go no matter who, how, and where it was coming from. I was done. I was ready to break free and simply move forward and never, ever look back.

AN INWARD CHANGE

"For I am the Lord, your God,
who takes hold of your right hand and says to you,
Do not fear; I will help you."

—Isaiah 41:13

In May 2006, the day after Audie's husband's birthday, he planned to travel to Atlanta, Georgia to visit his nephew. I drove him to the airport on Saturday morning, and he was to return on Monday evening. After dropping him off on Saturday morning, Audie called me that evening, letting me know that he had made it safely and that he and his nephew had gone to lunch and was planning events later that day. We talked again around 7:00 p.m. or so and agreed to talk again the next day on Sunday after church.

After cleaning the house and going to lunch with a friend, I came back home and just lounged around the house. A friend of mine had recently sent me a tape from her conference, which I spoke at just weeks prior, and I was listening to it.

The title of my subject was "God Has a Dream That Is Bigger Than You." Normally, I very rarely listened to myself on tape after a conference but I decided that day to do so. I was so glad that I did because it really ministered to me, and I was so excited about what God had used me to say to the ladies who attended.

After listening to the tape, I sat in my office and reflected on God's goodness. Normally, I could look out the front and see my flower bed from the formal dining room. However, this time, I thought something was wrong with my vision because this time, rather than seeing the flower bed or the streets, I saw what looked to be a steel ladder that was extremely tall. It was so tall I could not see the end just by simply looking up. I would have to back up quite a distance and then strain at that to see the end of the ladder in the sky.

The ladder was very narrow in size as if it was carved out to specifically fit one person to climb up. I remember getting up and going to the window to look out. It scared me. I returned to my seat and felt very uncomfortable about it, so I rubbed my eyes and kept them closed for a while and decided that I would try it again. However, when I opened my eyes and looked, it was still there—not naturally speaking but spiritually so. I cried out to the Lord in an audible voice and said, "What is this, Lord? Am I losing my mind?" As I continued to sit at the desk, I felt like I was watching a video tape of my own life.

I continued to stare at the ladder. Then I noticed what seemed to be a speck on the ladder high up in the sky. I could not visually make out exactly what appeared in the middle. So I inquired about what I was seeing. As if the speck was under a magnifying glass, the picture began to enlarge itself, and finally, I saw what it was. It was me with my head towards the earth and my feet in the opposite position on the ladder towards the sky. The ladder was very narrow in stature, and it was only room to fit the body perfectly; in other words, no room for error.

When I questioned the purpose of the view, the response that I received was, "Your positioning on the ladder indicates your dependence upon me. You are specifically positioned that way because if you try to look to your left or to your right for answers, directions, or guidance, you will not make it successfully. However, as you keep your focus and mind upon me by looking up, you will be alright that is why your head is pointed up to the sky." I finally understood. To God be the glory for his marvelous works! The vision left me drained and tired, so I sat on the couch and drifted off to sleep.

I woke up during the wee hours of the morning. A friend of mine had dropped by to spend the night and said that she had called at least twice and also ranged the door bell and knocked but still no answer from me. She was extremely worried about me because she did not understand what happened. I apologized and then went to bed.

The next morning, I was so very tired and almost did not make it to church but felt I needed to press my way instead. Upon arriving, I really wished that I had stayed home.

Something was missing. I felt drained and a little annoyed. An unsettling feeling was slowly creeping in. I just could not shake it to save my life. A friend of mine noticed my mood and asked me what was wrong, and I told her that something was happening somewhere, and it was happening to someone very close to me. However, I didn't know who or how to handle it. She said, "Let's go pray now. Come on, we'll go to the prayer room."

When we entered the prayer room, the woman began praying for me like never before. I was very moved by her compassion and sincerity during the prayer time. After the prayer, she walked me to the car and said, "Go home and get some rest." I drove home but didn't get any rest.

A couple of hours after I had made it home, I sat on the couch upstairs and laid my head back. Within a few minutes, the phone ranged distinctly with three short rings.

The caller would hang up, and the phone did this on three separate occasions. Annoyed, I said, "Who is doing this, and why won't they allow the phone to ring through without hanging it up and redialing?" The enemy spoke and said, "You're tired. Why don't you take a Tylenol and go lie down and get some rest." I remembered saying no to that immediately because I felt like I needed to stay up and be alert.

The phone ranged again, and this time I headed downstairs to answer it. Before I could reach the bottom of the stairs, I heard this voice in my spirit say, "When you answer it, it will be from your nephew telling you Audie is in the hospital." By the time I reached the bottom of the stairs, my feet feeling extremely light at this point, I heard my nephew's voice saying, "Heah, Auntie. This is Darrell, pick up, pick-up." I remember grabbing the phone and frantically saying hello when I heard a woman's voice, saying to the caller, "Who are you talking to? Is this his wife? Give me the phone, and you stay with him, I will talk to her."

Again, my heart beating fast, I said, "Hello, hello, who is this?" the woman said, "I am Mr. Murphy's doctor. Are you his wife?" I said, "Yes!" The doctor said, "I am going to try and make him comfortable until you get here." "Make him comfortable…until I arrive? What are you talking about?"

She said, "Your husband had a stroke and is paralyzed. His blood pressure is now at 278, and he is incoherent and is unable to speak or identify anyone." "Oh my god, please tell me this isn't happening to me!" Brenda screamed. The phone call was disconnected.

I remember going into our bedroom. I cried unto the Lord, "Please cover Audie in your blood. Keep him safe and in your care." What I remembered seeing next was one of the biggest Bibles I had ever laid my eyes on. This book was humongous. It was wide as an average door and equally as tall. This book was in my hands and my arms, and the pages were turning at a rapid rate of speed so quickly I could feel the wind blowing from the turn of each page.

As the pages turned, I was instantly reminded of each scriptural reference I ever learned or knew from childhood to current. Like, "The Lord is my shepherd I shall not want." Or "The Lord is my refuge and strength.

My very present help in the time of trouble." I was speed reading just to keep up. When I had apparently read or recited all that

I needed to know, the book closed automatically and disappeared without warning. Next, I went to my neighbor's house and told them what happened. They agreed to make travel arrangements for me while I called one of the deacons at the church.

After calling the church, countless people showed up and began to help me make sense out of everything. I only had a four-hour window to get packed and head out to the airport. Because Audie's phone was left at his nephew's house and everyone was at the hospital, I had no way to connect with anyone. I had no idea what airport to arrive at and who would be picking me up. Nevertheless, I kept packing. On the way to the airport, I was praying that God would keep my heart and my family. When I entered the airport, it was extremely quiet for a Sunday evening. There were very few people there.

I quickly found a seat and sat down. When it was time for me to take my flight, I was seated next to this very tall and big Texan gentleman, who said, "Hi, little lady! How are you this afternoon?" I greeted him and told him my story thus far. Without hesitation, he grabbed my hands, which dwarfed mine in size, and prayed a good old Texan prayer that made me smile and very grateful that I was sitting next to a believer.

I prayed, "God, I don't have to have a sentence from you just a single word will do for my situation to be forever changed. Just speak a word." With that, I heard in the spirit, "You need not travel as a wife, but as a servant to a servant." Instantly I was filled with God's amazing peace. I simply adjusted myself in my seat and enjoyed the flight.

My nephew picked me up at the airport totally nervous and visibly upset. He was ranting and raving because his favorite uncle was sick, and he felt helpless and probably scared as well. He drove like nobody's business to the hospital.

We talked a lot about God on the way. He asked question after question. I was not sure if he took in all the responses, but he asked the questions like he was extremely thirsty for knowledge and understanding right then and there. I smiled and told him it's going to be okay. He said to me, "How can you smile and not be crying right now?" Recognizing his fear, I took his hand and softly responded, "It's just Jesus!"

Upon arriving at the hospital at about 1:30 a.m., the two of us were greeted by a doctor in the lobby. She introduced herself as Audie's doctor on call for the evening. She led the way into the emergency room. The woman in the white coat had a very serious and concerned look on her face and appeared to be questioning herself as to how she was going to prepare me for the entry into Audie's room.

"Please follow me," she said. Taking that walk beside her was like walking the "green mile" for me. As I continued to pray with each stride in Jesus's name, I immediately felt strengthened. As we were about to enter Audie's room, the doctor asked me to wait so she could prepare the both of us.

Within a few minutes, she returned and asked me to follow. When the curtain was pulled back, there was my baby, totally clueless of who I was or why he was even there. My heart sunk immediately. But in the midst of it all, through the grace and mercy of Jehovah, I was more than able to hold my composure. Talking about leaning on the everlasting arms of Jesus, I called his name and simply rested in his presence.

Audie smiled at the doctor but immediately became puzzled and quiet when I called his name. He just simply starred at me. His smiled disappeared, and his eyes looked away from me as if he were ashamed that he didn't remember who I was or why I was there. It was clear he was struggling to try to remember where he must have known me from. I Whispered, "Jesus, help me bear this cross."

For the remainder of the night, I stood guard by Audie's bedside on hard, cold concrete flooring, singing to him and praying to God, "Watch over my baby and keep him covered under your blood." With each passing second, I continued to speak life over him. I kept repeating, "You shall live Audie and not die! God has a major work for you to do."

I recall standing for more than 6 hours on the hard concrete I stood on the hard concrete floor because there was no place to sit in Audie's make-shift hospital room watching carefully over him. Finally daybreak came both spiritually and naturally speaking, this was music to my ears. I could now hear noise in the hallways which indicated to me not only a new day dawning but that change was on the horizon; I braced myself for the news.

As I looked at my precious baby, I just knew that the journey before him would be tedious, but I had a strong foundation in my relationship with Jesus assuring me that he could be counted on as being an ever-present help and reliance in our time of trouble. In that moment, there was absolutely no doubt that both Audie and I were being clothed in his presence and that this too was going to pass.

About 6:30 a.m., the curtains were pulled back in Audie's makeshift room. A nurse entered to take Audie's vitals. After which, she said to me, "Mrs. Murphy, we are going to be moving Mr. Murphy in a few minutes to his private room." I thought to myself, With God all things are possible. We were now officially on our way into the journey before us. I remained focused and steadfast in God.

After getting Audie's private room, he still did not recognize me at all. I didn't push the issue. I adapted to his limitation of reasoning for the moment. It wasn't important to me that he couldn't recognize me, just as long as he knew that whoever I was, I was someone who obviously cared and loved him and stood vigilantly by his bedside.

Audie was taken from me the majority of the day for testing and retesting. I listened to reports over and over again about what his diagnoses were. Some were extremely negative and some were hopeful. No matter what, I knew that the real doctor had spoken and given his diagnoses. He shall live and not die, and I only needed to act in the realm of servanthood and not as a wife.

I spent the remainder of the day listening to God directing my steps and ministering to my mind. I felt his presence at all times. Around 3:00 p.m., Audie was returned to his room. I was told that he had swelling on the brain and that they were testing him to see if there was also blood there. I was informed that it was a possibility due to his blood pressure being 278 and the type of stroke that he had, he may not ever be able to speak again or remember. What they didn't know about me or Audie and the God that we served was that we believed the report of the Lord at all times.

While the doctors were giving me their medical diagnosis, I was thanking God privately that none of it were so. I continued to stand on the following Word of God:

> Surely he hath borne our griefs, and carried our sorrows: yet we did esteem him stricken, smitten of God, and afflicted. But he was wounded for our transgressions; he was bruised for our iniquities: the chastisement of our peace was upon him; and with his stripes we are healed. (Isa. 53:4–5).

> God is our refuge and strength, a very present help in trouble. (Ps. 46:1)

I decided to park and rest there in the spiritual realm because I had personally found that acknowledgement unto God is one way of measuring one's dependency upon the Almighty. When it comes to my pain, shame, hurt, woundedness, and rejection from others, I understood that I can come boldly and without hesitation to the throne and be opened about my nakedness. Although various people were calling and saying that they were praying for us, there were times, in that particular moment, I never felt so alone.

Stilling away for a moment of silence, I thought, here I am in Atlanta with limited funds in my pocket. A spouse who doesn't recognize me; a medical diagnosis that says Audie wouldn't make it. Limited family members to call upon while at the hospital and only a nephew and his wife in the general vicinity, I knew I had to lean and to depend solely upon God for added strength and He did not disappoint.

It was in those moments that I have personally found out that my faith was a muscle that I had to learn how to work and exercise every day. I grew more into who I was, whose I was, and who I belonged to in a matter of days; in the words of Zechariah 4:6, "'Not by might nor by power, but by my Spirit,' says the Lord Almighty."

Admittedly, at times, I wanted to walk away from the person I saw in the mirror because I deemed the cross I was trying to shoulder was too heavy for me to bear. However, I hadn't factor in the fact that it was in those precious moments when I heard the Spirit of the Lord whisper to me in my ear, "My daughter, it costs to follow Jesus. You have to be made."

I didn't fully grasp all that was taking place in my spiritual life because all I knew was that I truly loved God and only wanted to serve him. I thought no one would notice or care that I loved God with all my heart and soul by trying to remain under the spotlight and out of the public view. But it appeared that not only was that not the truth, but the more I praised God, sought to do his will and focused on him, the enemy pursued me and attempted to persecute me relentlessly.

There were some church people who asked, "Oh my god, Sister Murphy, I couldn't believe all this happened to you and your husband, I mean you are always talking about God and leading people into his presence, a leader in the church, I mean people look up to you and your husband and now all of this?"

These individuals didn't realize that leaders are not exempt from life's perils. That sooner or later in life, everyone gets a turn to suffer and endure hardship; however, the most vital point to remember is how one chooses to endure it is what matters most.

During the process of it all, when I didn't return phone calls as quickly, some accused me of being anti-social. Some wondered if we had lost our house and other material things. There were many times when I have felt so weak in my body and my heart ached from being persecuted, lied on, talked about, and disappointed by those who I really thought at least cared about me.

I have felt the pain of a broken heart and rejection. It is very sore and cold, but the Bible says, "He hath made us accepted in the beloved" (Eph. 1:6, KJV). It is also comforting to know that Jesus binds up the broken hearted, and heals their wounds, for He is the healing balm of Gilead.

I knew that Jesus has always stood by my side, when almost everyone else abandoned me. He has been my Redeemer, avenger, refuge, and my personal helper—always by my side. To those who may read this book, it is imperative that they fully embrace and understand this statement.

It is not enough to just familiarize yourself with verses and scriptures in the Bible turning to them only when trouble arise in your lives; but you must mediate upon the Word of God both day and night, being careful to remember that Jesus will never leave you not even for a fleeting moment, for he has promised us in Hebrews 13:5–6 (NIV), "Never will I leave you; never will I forsake us. You can say with confidence, The Lord is my helper; I will not be afraid."

Keeping the Word of God close to my heart kept me from becoming angry, frustrated, bitter, hateful, and resentful at others, including my own family. Instead I have learned to pray for all those who sit in judgment without any true wisdom of just what the others maybe going through in that moment. The other important thing as a reader of this book must keep in mind.

Another important factor to remember while going through personal trials and challenges is that absolutely no one in the world is exempt from daily trials, testing, and woundedness. It is important to understand that sometimes testing and tribulations come in waves and shifts. While you are feeling pressured from the frontline, someone is busy in the background, discrediting your name, position, and disposition.

There have been times when people have said things about me that were just uncalled for and caused great pain; however, I now know and have accepted that with every victory, I can expect direct and swift opposition because the devil would love nothing more than for me to simply just give up and turn back. Well, it is not going to happen. I have learned and I am sure that I still have a whole lot of more growing to do; even still daily, I have learned how to leave it all, including my heartaches and pain at the altar of God and to ask Him to fix it for me.

Back in the day, I was always trying to set the record straight and chase down every lie and liar. I wanted to know from them why were they lying on me and why were they bent and purposed on, causing me so much pain. What did I ever do to them for them to hate me so much?

One day, I wised up and am happy to report that I learned how to surrender myself at the altar of my Lord and Savior and ask God to create in me that clean heart and to renew in me that right spirit. Above all else, I asked God to give me wisdom of how to live day by day in him only. Most importantly, I want to know how to live at peace with my enemies daily. I believe that is when true release of unspeakable joy came into my heart and life.

I learned how to pray for every hater, every accuser, and abuser. In doing so, I gained more insight, strength, and peace for my personal journey. The Bible says in Matthew 5:44–45 (NIV), "From the very lips of Jesus Himself, 'But I say unto you, Love your enemies, bless those who curse you, do good to those who hate you, and pray for those who insult you and persecute you; That ye may be sons of your Father who is in heaven.'" One particular thing that I had to learn and still live by today is that we are only "human" and "No one is perfect," what we do not often give credence to is the understanding that each of us can give offense without knowingly understanding that we have truly hurt or wounded another.

However, by the same token it is a totally different story when the matter becomes a habit and deliberate choice to offend the other on a consistent basis and never give the matter a second thought. I am convinced that there are certain individuals who take earthly delight in hurting others at any cost.

I believe that it is in that moment that one must learn to "*trust in the Lord with all their heart and lean not on their own understanding, in all their ways submit to him, and he will make their paths straight*" (emphasis mine) (Prov. 3:5–6). All of my adult life, Audie and I have been givers throughout our marriage. We have often spent much of our twenties through our forties giving out to all in need whether their actual asking was a true need or want. We obliged anyway.

The majority of times in our giving sometimes never receiving anything back from those who constantly requested supposedly borrowing but never returning. Some actually stole, asked, and simply abused their daily, weekly, and yearly requests. Nevertheless Audie and I never stopped pursuing good over evil.

The funny thing about all this was sometimes in the midst of it all, there were some of the people in that very crowd who reaped and gained the most from us who sold us out and put their mouths on us to anyone in the world who dared to listened without blinking an eye.

In my effort to aid and assist some, there were times when I and my family were left with nothing and had to work two jobs just to make ends meet. The promise from others to borrow was never honored or acknowledged and may not have ever been the true intent in the first place. Still, but God…

However, what I now know for sure is that when I am seemingly left with nothing (tangible) that is, God is more than my enough. With him present in my life, I have absolutely everything that I need to start all over again never to return or remain in a world called lack. For God is truly my refuge and my strength, my very present help in times of trouble.

The Bible says in Isaiah 46:4 (NIV) "*I am he, who will sustain you. I have made you and I will carry you. I will sustain you and rescue you.*" What a timely word in this season or any season in your life. When God speaks, it is definitely over. No matter what the trial, testing, situation, circumstances, and problem. This is why it is critical for me to pray continuously over myself, family and others. Because sooner or later, there will come a time, as hard as it may be for people to grasp, that difficulties are going to arise.

When they do, one can only hope and pray that they will have, or at least know of, the one who can absolutely sustain them. So woe be unto that person who has not been a true friend, a good brother or sister, or even a good listener because although God is forever present, you still need and can benefit from the earthly help and shoulders of another.

It is vital to remember that there will be times of hardship and challenges. One may not even know where their next meal, dollar, or place to lay their head will come from. But just by the willingness to hold on and maintain the faith level in God, everything will be alright. I promise you when we learn to turn the page and enter into a new chapter in our lives with the help, guidance, and grace of God; we will find Jesus right there to help us with every step we take with or without the aid of others if necessary.

On the other hand, it very easy at times to allow the devil to steal, rent, borrow, or lease our joy. There are times when we do feel down and/or let down because of our circumstances, situations, or dilemmas. Remember the words of the Lord, which states, "When you pass through the waters, I will be with you; And through the rivers, they shall not overflow you. *"When you walk through the fire, you shall not be burned, nor shall the flame scorch you*" (Isa. 43:2).

The second day while Audie was still in the hospital in Atlanta, the Lord led me to sing to him, read to him and to continually pray over him. At this point, I became his earthly covering, and I gladly accepted the opportunity to do so. Slowly but surely as he began to warm up to me, I would read various things to him and ask him to repeat it to me, and he would. Then I would make a game out of the reading materials.

When I sat on his bed and we would played card games, I always made it interesting. Even though Audie still didn't recognize who I was by day two, I sensed he recognized my spirit and became at ease and comfortable with me being near him. He began to smile more.

Every now and then, he would gesture for me to come closer to him and maybe hold his hand. That was very special and memorable to me. By day three, Audie woke up and pulled back the covers. He looked at me and got out of bed. He got out of bed! A man, who had been declared paralyzed and possibly would never walk again, simply got out of bed on day three, walked himself to the bathroom, no problems at all. He went into the bathroom, closed and locked the door, took his own shower, combed his hair, brushed his teeth and returned to his bed.

He still was not talking but otherwise looked his old self without any signs of sickness anywhere in his body. In fact, his nurses questioned why he was there in the first place. They wondered why this woman is here, ordering his food for him, cutting up his food for him, and answering most of the questions for him. He looked perfectly fine. I gently explained to the nurse what had actually happened to him, and they were shocked and dismayed.

From day three, the Lord continued to heal Audie's body, and now he was talking to me. He remembered me, and his progress was moving rapidly. By the time that he saw his doctor again, it would be day four, and Audie was well on his way to a full recovery. The doctor showed up around 5:00 p.m. with therapist in tow. As he was discussing the negative report on Audie, which included a bunch of cannots, Audie suddenly looked at him then at me. He rose from bed and said, "I'm fine." The doctor went white.

The doctor, gaining his composure, asked Audie to walk to the door. But first they had to put a gate belt on him, and when they did, Audie sat up in the bed, put on the belt, hopped off the bed, and did his swagger to the door and back without the slightest limp whatsoever. The doctor said, "Can you touch your nose?" Oliver touched his nose, eyes, lips, and cheeks.

"Was there anything else?" Audie asked. The doctor got up, turned around, and said, "How long have this been happening?" My response was since day three. The doctor simply opened up the door and walked out never to be seen again.

Audie and I never physically saw the doctor again but just received discharged paperwork through his nurse that he was to remain in the hospital for another couple of days and be discharged.

The doctor did not want Audie flying so we could only travel by ground transportation. From that, I would have to drive some eighteen hours back to Fort Worth. When I came to Atlanta, the individual who made the flight registration for me only purchased a one-way ticket at the cost of $650.00, so I was stuck in Atlanta.

We thought we would have to rent a car and somehow come up with enough money for gas to drive back home. But for the grace and mercy of God, there were those praying for us in Fort Worth that were sending the rescue team in to pick us up and bring us back home.

The people who came for were angels sent and directed by God. To say they were an unusual pair is an understatement. They handled Audie and I with kid gloves. Every need was met and then some.

Not one stone was unturned and we were truly blessed beyond measure. The church surprised us and made us proud. Audie eventually became strong enough to attend therapy five days a week for approximately four months. In the meantime, I took off two months for family leave act (FMLA) to take care of him.

RETURNING INTO BATTLE

"Come to me, all you who are weary and burdened,
and I will give you rest."

—Matthew 11:28

After that time off, I returned back to work and found out that I had been moved to a different team—a team of thirty-five representatives in the balance transfer queue as opposed to the original twelve I was previously assigned to. Actually I now had more representatives than anyone in the entire call center, and my supervisor's expectations of me were even higher. Even though my boss was praising the fact that my quality scores exceeded expectation, he never once came through on his promises to the team or me as a leader of that team once those percentages were exceeded which were often.

Nevertheless, my team and I kept our heads up and or our focus on what was important, and we moved forward. Eventually, I registered for classes at the Southwestern Seminary Theological College in Fort Worth. I learned a great deal. For starters, it is not a school for the faint hearted, and one really must search deep inside to see what it takes to become a missionary and a follower of Christ and what it means to be a servant of the God Most High.

I witnessed on many occasions those who sold all that they had to go to foreign countries and witness Christ to others who may not otherwise ever would have an opportunity to hear about

his name at all. These individuals were very passionate and determined men and women, didn't allow anyone or anything to get in
their way of their call. I was most inspired and impressed by their
desire to make a difference in the world.

I have always been a person who had a desire to serve God
with my whole heart, mind, and soul. I honestly live to make an
impact in the lives of others around me. I had to learn was that
sometimes in the process of trying to help others, there will be
those in the crowd who will come along just to pull all of your
ideas, vision, strength, energy and joy only to leave you depleted
and dissolved of happiness if you allow it.

There were many days; I had to steal away like David, who
prayed, "Return unto me the joy of your salvation" (Ps. 55:12,
KJV). Remember these words also from Nehemiah 8:10 (NIV),
"For the joy of the Lord is your strength." He is my strength
when I am weak. He is the up lifter of my head. As the Bible says
so powerfully in Psalm 18:1–3 (NIV):

> I love you, O Lord, my strength. The Lord is my rock, my
> fortress and my deliverer, my God is my rock, in whom I
> take refuge. He is my shield and the horn of my salvation,
> my stronghold. I call to the Lord, who is worthy of praise,
> and I am saved from my enemies.

From time to time, I would often have individuals personally
approach me and ask why I took my walk with God so seriously.
In a lot of ways, my walk with Christ to them was misinterpreted
that perhaps I may have attempted to be or to act like something
I should not have. Others were quick to judge and say mean,
hateful, and hurtful words and comments just because I believed
the Word of God for my life.

I was neither deterred nor distracted by my haters or enemies.
I continued to believe, receive, and grow in my relationship with
God. Each and every day, I was well aware that I was blessed to
witness another dawning and could never allow it to be taken

for granted no matter who did not think that it was appropriate. I thanked God daily and would be found saying, "Lord, how I thank you that you have allowed it to be so. Now, what is it about this day that you have designed for me to do?"

For years I had unknowingly allowed the enemy through others to restructure my right as a daughter of the God Most High to choose joy over sadness for myself. I didn't understand why people would choose to scandalize my name rather than to speak words of kindness and if nothing else, how about just tell the truth.

It was mind boggling to me that some people, no matter nationality, creed, and color, rich or poor, would rather criticize rather than celebrate the true joy of another. The Bible declares, *"For as he thinketh in his heart, so is he: Eat and drink, saith he to thee; but his heart is not with thee"* (Prov. 23:7, KJV).

After working for the call center for more than eight years, the day came for my departure to launch out in to the deep where I believed God was calling me. I made up my mind to follow hard after His will for my life, and I was never more satisfied. It did not matter how I served—whether it was through conferences, preaching the gospel, or teaching—as long as I had the opportunity to share the Word of God wherever I went. Daily, I would eat, sleep, dream, imagine, and live ministry.

I had probably preached more sermons in my sleep than when I was actually awake. I soaked up the Word of God. It provided nutrients, balance, substance, support, direction, and guidance for my life. I needed God like a druggie needed his absolute high probably more so.

In those final days of working for the call center, I knew that I did not want to continue my tenure there. Every day I would pray to God to please show me what was next. After my first conference, I was absolutely convinced that leaving was the vein that God wanted me to flow in. By my tenth conference, I didn't look back. I was sold out. The cost of following him didn't matter any longer because I was truly in love way over my head, and I no longer cared who judged, criticized, or hated me for it. After all, I had the King of kings and Lord of lords on my side.

The days leading up to my final days at work, I absolutely dreaded going to work with every fiber of my being. I would wake up in the morning in tremendous pain from the crown of my head to the very soles of my feet and go to sleep at night asking God to change me and to order my steps. I could feel the tug on my heart and soul that clearly this assignment was up and it was time to go. I went to work extremely stressed, worn down, sleep deprived, and overwhelmed. My eating habits were extremely poor. I was allowing people, church and all, to pull me in fifty different directions.

One of the most vital lessons that I learned was the importance of knowing when someone is courting me the whole person or attempting to pimp me for my gift and favor that I had with God and man only. There were some invitations that came with attachments and certain criteria. It was either man's way or no way, meaning that you most likely would not be invited back again.

I knew right then and there, unless I learned this lesson, I would forever be hurt, wounded, or quite frankly, left for spiritually dead many of day's long after the event was over. Thank God, I know that the Bible says in Exodus 15:26 (NIV), "For I am the Lord, who heals you."

To the readers of this book, I can attest to many days of running to the Lord for healing, security, covering, divine protection, and just to be kept by the master. Whenever I needed healing, I would go to the Lord. Whenever my heart was aching, I would go to the Lord; whenever I felt weak, I would go to the Lord.

In everything and anything, I now go to the Lord—no questions asked. Whenever someone asked me how I became so strong in the Lord, my immediate response to them was, "My friend, keep living and loving God, and I promise you your response will change sooner rather than later. You too will be running to him for coverage as well." As the Bible says in Psalm 46:1 (KJV), "God is our refuge and strength, a very present help in trouble."

On my final day with the company, the closer I got to the door leading to the outside world, the more my heart leaped for joy.

I could almost smell freedom and deliverance being just around the corner; and at that moment, it smelled extremely sweet. Even though my job provided limited earthly security, it was not the security that I truly needed.

The more I hung on to this job for the paycheck and the false security, the more hell, persecution, crazy customers, lewd remarks, ill-equipped bosses who were managers in theory but not necessarily indeed.

There were days I knew all too well that had it truly not been for grace and mercy, I would have lost my everlasting mind. I was tired coming and going. Most days, wounded going and coming, overworked going and coming and many days I had coworkers asking me to work their shifts, promising to make it up later, which never happened.

Not only were they at ease with lying, but some of them went on to become lying coaches in their professional fields. They didn't have a problem with me taking their escalated callers, dealing with irate, unprofessional customers, unlearned human beings who possessed no morals, characters, or at times "human-ness" by the way they talked to another human being. They just simply passed the buck, often with no repercussions.

During this period in my life, I gained more weight than I had ever weighed in my life. I was barely sleeping. Although I lay down nightly, I wasn't resting. It didn't matter if I was at work two to three hours early. I was always called upon by managers, peers, and employees to take escalated calls one right after another, while others ran the other way, looked the other way, or simply got out of the way.

There would be days I would go without lunch or a break. My back and feet ached terribly. My feet swelled, and I was always extremely tired and desperately ready for change at any cost. So I prayed and prayed until true deliverance came. As I walked outside, knowing that it was my last day in prison, I wanted to literally start singing across the parking lot, "Free at last, free at last, thank God almighty, I am truly free at last." I got in my vehicle and never looked back. That chapter in my life was done! Praise him!

BRIGHTER DAYS AHEAD

"And my God will meet all your needs according to his glorious riches in Christ Jesus."

—Philippians 4:19

In the days ahead, rather than focus on what I thought I would miss, I became more interested in what lied ahead for me. I knew that I would not miss the large team I had, the outrageous phone calls, my enormous workload, and the additional workloads of others. I wouldn't miss the endless deadlines with no real purpose or reasoning. I wouldn't miss the phony people who smiled so diligently in my face and carried and used the daggers with a dual purpose for my back and sometimes my face, only to deny their actions later when questioned.

That decision to leave was the best decision that could have ever been made. It provided instant peace and much-needed rest and relaxation that I needed to become recharged and focused for my real purpose.

Within the month, I travelled to Tulsa, Oklahoma, to a women's conference in which I was one of the primary speakers; my topic, ironically, was Jeremiah 29:11: "'For I know the plans I have for you,' declares the Lord, 'plans to prosper you and not to harm you, plans to give you hope and a future.'" How ironic for this topic at this specific time in my personal life when I needed directions the most.

During that event, God showed me how the people in that story wanted his blessings and assurance; the problem was they didn't want the giver of the blessing or his guidance or direction. Just bless us Lord and leave us alone. That phrase ranged familiar with me because of the way as a people our reaction is to what God has called us to do. We want him but we never want to commit.

God wanted to show the people that from the very beginning, he already made the perfect plans for their lives. He had already laid the perfect foundation for their lives, but they would not be able to possess that aspect without him being at the helm of their lives; therefore, they could not just receive the blessings without accepting him also. The Lord was being more than generous.

Interestingly enough, while I was attending that conference, I was introduced to a woman who I later invited to speak at my next conference in the spring. We exchanged personal information and kept in touch off and on. However, it was during one of our many telephone conversations that I realized I had actually made a huge mistake by asking her to speak at the conference.

The more I spoke with this woman, the more I realized that we were not on the same page or the heartbeat of where Innovative Ministries, Inc. was going. Perhaps this woman's own personal hidden agenda for coming was entirely the wrong motive.

When I realized that I had made the mistake, there was nothing that I could do to undo it. I knew it was going to cost me dearly. Every time I tried to un-invite the woman, she was persistent in her attempt to come even as busy as she pretended that her schedule was. Looking back on that time, I know that it was a mistake I regret even to this day.

Not only was this person's heart not true to my ministry, but it played out in public while she was standing before the people. She did everything within her power to make me and the people in attendance look and feel badly; however, the enemies' attempts were quickly shut down, and she was sent packing never to return. Thank God for discernment.

Little did I know that she had a friend who kept challenging her to ask for certain outrageous things before and during the conference; they talked prior to the conference after she had gotten off her flight all the way to my home, and during the whole time-frame that she was in my home, they never ceased to stop plotting about what to ask for in terms of perks.

Instead of coming down to be with all of the presenters and the actual conference attendees, she preferred to stay locked up in her private room until it was her "turn" to speak. After her friend finished singing and gave her testimony, she finally showed up looking totally disinterested in the entire event.

When she did get up to speak, her approach was anything but compassionate and godly. She actually started her "talk" by insulting the musicians, asking them to stop playing. She then unleashed her tyrant spirit upon the praise team and said that I was too easy going and would not speak up for myself but that she didn't have a problem with doing so.

She disrespected the women who attended the conference and me as well. She talked more about herself, her ministry, and her J. C. Penney's clothing. Not only was I and the entire audience shocked at her behavior, but her demeanor and lack of respect for the people of God was absolutely appalling to say the least.

Not only did this woman return to my home after the conference but she continued to talk with my family and friends about her negative thoughts toward her personal lack of consideration while she attended the conference.

When the individual that I thought I knew got back home, she had the audacity to call me and say, "You didn't even call me to make sure that I made it home safely." Mind you, this is a person, who invited herself, shared the hotel room with this woman, and rearranged the already original plans that I had previously made, which costs me more money.

Other conferences followed, and life moved forward for me. Every now and then I would get a call from the two ladies pretending that they were absolutely clueless about why things turned out between us as they had. One of the ladies had the nerve to say, "Brenda, if I have done anything wrong, it is your responsibility to let me know. I mean I won't know unless you told me."

My response after I finished laughing was, "Really? Honestly, could you really be that clueless? I never would have imagined that. Your underhandedness seems to come so effortlessly. I can tell you do this often."

Determined to move forward and be free of hypocrites, I decided to start over fresh. In 2008, Audie and I after much prayer and fasting decided to leave our current church and move in the direction we felt God leading us to go. After visiting various churches for approximately six months, we finally settled on one in particular. We truly believe that it was definitely the move of God that led us there.

In September 2008, I began taking online courses for my degree in business. In December 2009, I found a part-time job with a five-star hotel in downtown Fort Worth. I took a part-time position as a barista in their local Starbucks coffee shop, where I truly enjoyed daily interactions with various customers.

During the early stages of employment with the hotel, it was early mornings and late nights. I remembered vividly how long the lines use to be daily. For me, customer service was endless both day and night. People from all over came from near and far for the good coffee, to fraternize, socialize and even to look alive. (I had to throw that in.)

It was a lot of work before the grand opening, and certainly thereafter was pure madness. Never in my life could I have envisioned wearing an orange-yellow street vests, combat boots, goggles, and blue jeans to work. I honestly looked like I was going to be directing traffic on 635 in Dallas somewhere. Each night when I got home after work, I had to brush the dust out of my hair and wipe the dust out of her goggles.

My boots looked like I had just finished the last leg of my course through Egypt, and my body ached from head to toe. Not one stone or joint was left untouched. I spent my first two months of employment in total disbelief and utter shocked that I would allow myself to be talked and almost coerced into taking what I thought then as a godforsaken job. Even during the training period, I thought this has nothing to do with ministry.

During our introduction of everyone, the employees were asked to tell at least three things about themselves after the basic "hello my name is…" I really tried not to say much. In fact, I didn't want them to know anything about my ministry at all. I figured if I made it through orientation, the subject could possibly be revisited but only if and when it was appropriate to do so. In the weeks and months that follow, I cried each night that I went home from work, asking God, "What is this?" Sadly, this behavior went on for about three more months.

I could have heard them a mile away saying, "Oh my Lord, is that Sister Murphy in here? What on earth are you doing working in Starbucks? While they were talking to me, they were monitoring me from head to toe with the most ungodly look on their faces. Not only was I working in a fast-service coffee shop, I was required to stand for a minimum of eight hours a day.

My heart skipped a beat at the mere thought that I would have to stand for that long. I didn't know a single person that did that for a living and all I could think of was horses enjoy standing. That wasn't even the kicker. Once we got the store up and organized, the employees were responsible for ordering all supplies, keeping the store stocked, restocking during store hours, making sure it was clean at all times, above all making each customer's day a great out of body experience. Emphasis mine!

Then came the wonderful day everyone looked so forward to—payday. When I got my first paycheck, I nearly fainted never to return back to the land of the living. I thought if this is a joke, then it is a really cruel joke and someone has deliberately played an evil trick to say the least. For all the long hours that I had put in including the weekend, I didn't even bring home enough to make Snoopy's pet a lunch, and he doesn't require much.

Shocked, upset, and in total denial all in the same day, I went home took a shower and went straight to bed. I didn't have the energy to pass go. I figured if I went home and slept it off; the bad dream would be over before it became a total nightmare. When I woke up, the nightmare still remained a constant. "Lord," I cried, "what happened, and why was I back in Egypt? Did the bus, train, plane take a wrong turn? Help me!"

I was working and attending school full-time at that time. I was averaging three classes and two of them had to do with math. During those times I wanted to go out back and build myself a personal altar and just lay on it for days chanting, "Come now, Lord, come now."

I thought whose life is this because it cannot be mine. Daily Audie tried to encourage me, counsel me and pray for me, I was sure he may have thought to himself, "Now, Lord, whatever you are doing in the life of my wife, could you please do it as quickly as possible because I cannot take any more."

For the five years that I worked for this five-star hotel, I opened for them at 5:00 a.m., which meant my day started at 3:00 a.m., leaving the house at 4:30 a.m. to get to work and start setting up the store. No two mornings began the same. Some days it would be rainy and cold, dark and rainy, muggy, or occasionally, a breeze would blow through. At any rate, it was still 4:30 a.m. when all the crazies, creeps, muggers, rapists, winnows, perverts, and what have you were out and about.

There wasn't any close range parking that didn't cost you your blood, sweat, tears, and a down payment on your first born; therefore, you had to walk through the fire and brimstone to get to your place of employment. Getting there safely at 4:30 a.m. was nothing short of a miracle in itself. Often on my journey through early morning "Egypt," I would encounter drunks that reeked of alcohol and cigarettes. I saw many sleeping on park benches and asleep standing up next to the little trees in the park.

There were cabbies waiting for a passenger or whatever, and then there was me, the woman who walked with her head held high, prayer in her heart, cell phone and Mace in hand should anything inappropriate happen.

After reaching work safely, I forgot I still had my Mace in my pocket when my boss at the time, along with a police officer, noticed it. He pulled me aside and said, "Brenda, what on earth do you have in your pocket?" To which I replied, "Mace." "What?" they replied. "Why? You are fully aware as discussed in the orientation employees are not allowed to carry such things on their persons on the floor. Now, can you please explain yourself?"

"Sure," I happily replied with a major grin on my face. "My feet were burning, my back felt like I had two small unidentifiable animals riding on my spine each time I moved, explain yourself?" I have been standing now without a break of any kind for more than five hours, no lunch in sight, and you want to know why I have a can of mace on me? Well, let's see, which one of you would choose to walk through Egypt at 4:30 a.m. on any day, risking your life to get to work and when you meet Mr. Robber, Mr. Rapist, or Mr. Thrill Seeker, at best, the most you can say is please don't kill, rob, or rape me this morning, I am trying my best to get to work and punch in on time.

But need I digress; the real reason why I carry this Mace is because I cannot afford an Uzi right now. They cleared their throats and backed away. I can only assume the subject matter was closed for discussion since it was never brought again in my presence.

Working at this hotel, I met a lot of interesting, motivating, kind, and compassionate people; some of which I am assured I will never see again in this life but that's okay. They were vital for me to interact with at the time, and it was necessary for our paths to cross in that moment. The connection that our spirits matched in those minutes possessed enough synergy that propelled me to move forward even when I didn't know exactly how I was going to get to that next level, or even if that next level was possible for me to achieve.

One day while setting up the store at 5:00 a.m., I felt the power of God move over me like nothing before. I stopped everything I was doing in that instance and began to worship him in the midst of setting up the display case and getting ice for the dispenser. I was very familiar with the voice of God and readily heeded what he had to say. I didn't care who might walk in or what was happening on the outside of the room. All I knew was that he cared enough about me in that hour to show up and visit with me, to counsel me and to give me a word in due season.

I wasn't concerned about my past or what might happen today at work. I was not even concerned about my present situation or my circumstances at the moment. I knew all too well that when God shows up, everything else pales in comparison. In fact, nothing else, mattered because in that moment alone, change had just showed up; and when that transpires, all I needed to do was shift with it. Praise God!

As I began to worship and praise God, I knew that something bigger than me was happening. I was instantly becoming anew, alive and full of possibilities. I knew that God was dealing with me in my now and not in my past.

In that moment, I realized God cared enough about me to show up and affect my atmosphere right down to what mattered to me most. He could care less about my emotions being disturbed, or what my circumstances were attempting to dictate to me, because He being God and Lord over my life had already ordered my steps and set the plan for my life in motion over two thousand years ago. All he was asking me to do in that brief moment was to believe that all things in my now were possible.

Not only did I believe in Jehovah but my whole mentality shifted. The Spirit of the Holy Ghost spoke, "Brenda, if you can just get over yourself, I will show you great and mighty things to come. You are being placed here in this role not for the money or the lack thereof but to be a witness to those who may or may not know me. Those who have never heard of me, or for those who do not believe that I can do all things but fail!

This assignment is not even directly about you. Although, it affects you indirectly, it is not about you but for those you will encounter who will recognize that I live through you and will desire to come closer to me as a result."

It was in that moment that I realized that if I were to move into my God-given destiny, the final word over my life had to come from my lips. I had to agree with God that I was going to become everything that He had ordained for me to be and that out of my mouth; I must command those gifts and talents that were lying dormant in my life to rise up and live.

I had to declare life over everything that interested me and that were vital to my survival to come forth in the name of Jesus. Not tomorrow, but today. I began to speak life over my health, family, finances, ministry, and the things that mattered most to me. I had to learn to ignore what the bank records said and see myself being debt free, and the list continued. I was not just saying a bunch of words hoping that the debt just disappeared on its own. I did my part in the process and God honored it all because of his faithfulness.

The Word of God declares in James 4:3, "You ask and do not receive, because you ask with wrong motives, so that you may spend it on your pleasures." In other words, whinnying won't move the hand of God. Crying and having temper tantrums doesn't get it. Having a nervous breakdown doesn't get it.

Feeling pity or self-loathing won't get it either. Speaking negative thoughts over your life or allowing others to chime in won't do. One must take a good, hard, and necessary look at themselves in the spiritual mirror and declare once and for all that the person they are seeing standing before them today is an overcomer in Jesus's name. They have the power and have been empowered to change their situation by the decision making of their mind.

True change only comes about when one decides that they are ready to move forward. That decision does not and often will include others; however, it begins with the person. Your family may feel like you have lost your everlasting mind or that they are not going with you. Your spouse may say, "Yeah right, baby, you go right ahead and make it happen. I'll be here when you finish but I ain't going with you."

Your co-workers may say it can't be done. But I double dog dare you to ask God, the one who holds the plan for your life, what his thoughts towards you are and to step out in that realm in which you heard his specific word for your life. You will never be the same from that time forward.

You cannot wait until you see the fruition of the dream come true first. You must learn to leap in what you believe God's purpose is for your life without asking others to touch and agree with you all the time. Stop asking others about what you should do because sometimes others are hard pressed to see only what they want to see in you and that depends on how their day or life is going at the moment.

That morning, I had to declare that I was everything that God had breathed into me not just that day but over two thousand years ago. It was imperative that I remembered that I was the head and not the tail. I was the whole and the healed of God.

I was the lender and not the borrower. I wasn't a Starbucks barista just created to sweep a floor, greet the customers, make the coffee, serve pastries, prepare sandwiches, and make various drinks. That was an assignment, not the purpose of my life.

That position only served as a conduit for which God would use his spirit to pass through to me and make right connections with those who would assist me in getting to the next lesson, assignment, or level of completion.

FINISHING WHAT I STARTED

"When he has brought out all his own,
he goes on ahead of them, and his sheep follow him
because they know his voice."

—John 10:4

For every negative person I met, or negative experience I received in any given day, I asked God to turn it around so I could use it for my personal good. I asked him to help me not dwell in the land of self-pity or woe is me. I remembered when I decided to go back to school and finish the degree plan that I started, there were some who doubted me, talked about me and even questioned my reasoning for doing so.

They asked me, "Why are you doing that now in your life? Isn't that very expensive to go back to school? How are you going to pay for that?" I had only one simple answer: His name is Jesus! And he makes all things new!

One thing that is exceptionally necessary for the journey I believe in life is purpose, drive, willingness, tenacity, focus, prayer, patience, compassion, faith, and dedication. If you are expected to move forward and get pass obstacles, naysayers, non-believers, haters and the lack, sometimes you have to do battle with yourself and say, "Not today. Today, I am not going to buy into my own self-criticism or put-downs." I choose to move forward.

Today, I choose not to revisit memory lane trying to remember every time I tried and failed or how many doors were closed in my face when I tried this or that. I didn't keep personal score of how many times certain relationships I may have encountered failed or how many people had walked out of my life within the past year or so. I had decided that the God that I served was more than enough to make all the difference in the world to me. I decided that I was not going to worry or fret about what I did not have; rather, I thanked God for what I did have in my possession.

I made up my mind that I was no longer going to cry about the spilled milk from the glass but rather rejoice over the milk that remained in the glass. For those who chose not to celebrate my God-given gifts, talents, anointing or friendship, I declared that I would simply move on and thank God for each new day being honored to be in His will.

In my opinion, it no longer mattered who was happy for me or not. By now, I had learned how to celebrate my own victories alone if necessary. I have decided to no longer wait for those who may or may not want to celebrate me, who doesn't have time to share in my happiness. I was going to move forward and be a blessing to others who have fallen prey to the enemies same old tactics as I once allowed myself to do.

I realized that I must continue to move forward with or without others being a part of my triumphs. I understand that I can do badly all by myself, and I don't need anyone pushing me down to do so. But I would welcome someone truly encouraging me to move up. I have made a decision to stop crying over and about people who were not crying over me. I can no longer concern myself with those who do not want me to succeed. I have stopped worrying about why they don't call, won't return my calls. In the words of one of my friends, "I am over it already."

I was learning to push past old things that use to slow me down. Things that used to cause me to sit down, turn around, and stay down. I was learning that things, issues, and circumstances are merely stepping stones used as windows of opportunities to build upon if I am willing to do the work it takes to make it happen.

Now I am asking God for wisdom and not just basic common sense because I know that "ye are of God, little children, and have overcome them; because greater is he that is in you, than he that is in the world" (1 John 4:4, KJV). Overcoming my past is not easy to do but it is doable. It is possible. Only believe and keep the faith and this too shall past.

As I continued to work at Starbucks, one day during a snow storm (yes snow storm in Fort Worth, Texas), one of the customers who had been frequenting the store ever since it opened came over for his usual drink of a tall latte with raspberry syrup and a heated pastry, engaged me in conversation. While they were talking, I mentioned to him that I was taking online courses and that I was getting ready to do my internship in human resources and asked if he knew of a place where I could do this.

He said, "Here, take my card and send me your resume," He then left. I continued to work and placed the card in my apron. I didn't look at it again for another three to four days before I remembered him doing so.

When I did look at the card, it listed him as the human resources director at the college. God is good! And the rest was history. Working there allowed me to expand my work experiences, gain a greater insight into the world of human resources, as well as meet new contacts and network. Overall, it was a challenging but interesting timeframe in my professional and personal experience.

While enjoying the benefits of working for both these very different yet powerful corporations, my family and I were hit again by the unimaginable. After working for a powerful corporation for over eighteen years as a tariff manager in the regulatory department, Audie was laid off due to tenure on the job in October of 2011. At the same time, my beloved brother Otha passed away in Detroit, Michigan, and his body was brought back home where he grew up for burial. He was buried in the same cemetery as our dad and other loved ones. Like all other life concerns, we dealt with them and moved forward.

In December, I was invited back to my home town to preach at my old church. Being assured that I had heard from the Lord, I didn't waiver in my approach when the Lord gave me the topic of "The Church Moving Forward, Take Your Rightful Position." In that message, I believe that it didn't necessarily just apply to "church" people parse, but to those individuals who were a part of the body of Christ, making up their minds to follow Christ in their individual assignments.

The Word of God was strong in saying that whatever role or position God had called the body of Christ to, we, as people of God, are to be diligent in our approach toward getting the assignment done; because no man knows for sure when the Son of Man will come. The body of the church must take heed to the attitude most church people share today.

At times, we can be lackadaisical about our approach in dealing with ministry as a whole. If we don't like or care for the assignment, we tend to handle it in a nonchalant manner. In other words, we do the assignment halfway without any real passion or rush.

For many, the approach to ministry is done as a showmanship and not a privilege to truly serve God. We show up just to be seen rather than to do the work he has called us to do. Some churches have reduced their praise and worship into an all-out competition at best, and no real worship is ever formed. I admit that on many levels, I have witnessed this on too many occasions.

Sadly enough for some, they seemingly have ran without the true vision or the mission and purpose why they accepted the assignment in the first place. The Word of God doesn't lie. In the Bible, we are warned that:

There will be terrible times in the last days. People will be lovers of themselves, lovers of money, boastful, proud, abusive, disobedient to their parents, ungrateful, unholy, without love, unforgiving, slanderous, without self-control, brutal, not lovers of the good, treacherous, rash, conceited, lovers of pleasure rather than lovers of God—having a form of godliness but denying its power. Have nothing to do with such a people. (2 Tim. 3:1–5)

Point taken! That statement alone has covered every conceivable concept one can think of, yet there are very few changes seemingly made in the hearts of man today.

Anyway, after returning home, I heard through the proverbial grapevine that for some of the people, they didn't think too highly of the message and probably not even of the deliverer of the message; however, I learned early on that if I were too remotely stand a chance in preaching the gospel, I had better learn to wear thick skin well and not take it personally because if people won't hear Jesus, they definitely won't want to listen to me when it comes to the gospel, even when it is written before their eyes.

Audie and I returned home not too wounded, praise God. We have learned not to dwell in any particular moment too long, especially if it is negative because it will only serve to bring us down, make us angry, or simply take our focus off the real truth, which is God's truth.

And at the end of the day, nothing else really mattered. Upon returning home, we decided to ride the rest of the year out just being grateful and thankful for all that God had done for us and our families, friends, and community. Just to give him thanks in all things no matter what because he truly didn't have to do it but he did was our only main objective.

IF GOD BE FOR ME, WHO CAN BE AGAINST ME?

In January 2012, we started off with challenges but kept our heads high and chose to stay positive. We noticed right around March, opposition seemed to be coming from all areas, and they were relentless in their approach. Sadly enough, not all the opposition came from the outside, but some direct hits came from within the family. At first, we thought it was by sheer coincidence, and perhaps, by mistake that our names kept being used in such an unlikely, unflattering manner. But one thing lead to another, then another, and then we had to face the facts. No, this was all intentional.

The spiritual warfare had been planted, and I and my family were now considered the direct target of specific bullets and weapons. Boy did they hurt, injure, and sting. Reeling from one insult, to a lie, from a backbiting situation to something else, I realized that I needed to take cover under the wings of the Almighty if I and my family were to withstand these ungodly tests.

In April, the heat was turned up even more against me and my family by immediate family members. Flaming arrows were approaching from all directions. The sad thing about the false disclaimers, were no one bothered to see if any of the gossiping or lies were remotely true. At best, it was a lot of heresy that came from one source who took pleasure in spreading the discord throughout various topics of conversations.

Bewildered from all this, I made a conscious effort to stop everything and personally shut everything down and turn my face and my concerns unto the Lord. I called upon the Lord for all it was worth, and I didn't let up until I clearly heard from him.

I deliberately chose to dig in my heels and not let go until there were answers and direction. I had made up my mind like Job: "Though he slay me, yet will I trust in him: but I will maintain mine own ways before him" (Job 13:15). And if that meant I would lose everyone that I thought was previously for me, I was not turning back or selling out for what I knew was right and true in Jesus's name.

Months rolled on, and Audie was doing fine. He applied for several part-time positions and eventually took a position with the Fort Worth transportation authority department.

The job schedule was brutal and extremely taxing on his time and his health. For instance, Audie had to often report to work at insane hours of 3:30 a.m. and work until sometimes 3:00 p.m. without official breaks and lunches. If someone else did not show up for work or was running late for their shift, Audie had to pick up their slack.

This job being something totally out of the ordinary from any other job he has ever had to work was strenuous for him. He still hung in there and tried his best to make it work for the sake of his family's well-being. That is one of the many things that I love about my husband. He is good to his family at all times. No matter what, he takes his role seriously and guards the door well. I totally respect that about him. He is definitely my godly covering.

Months past, and Audie passed all his testing for the transportation department and moved forward. About a week or so before his ninety days was up on the job, he was asked to work on a Sunday morning and to report around 11:00 a.m., and he did so. He was both excited and adamant about attending the early service and wanted me to join him. His face lit up the Saturday before, and all that he could talk about was seeing and hearing our bishop preach on Sunday morning. He was so excited about having the day off and being a part of his church family.

On Sunday morning, we got up, got dressed, had breakfast together, and headed out the door for church. Upon arrival, to church, Audie was still on a spiritual high—he was singing, laughing, and just excited about the Lord and his relationship with God. After we arrived at church, Audie who is a very friendly out-going person did his usual meet and greet and sat about two rows behind me since he had to leave the service early for work didn't want to be a distraction to anyone. Just before he left, he asked someone to touch me so I'd look back, and he blew me a kiss. He gave me his "Audie smile" and said, "I love you baby, I'll see you tonight."

We both assumed that he would be home around 2:00 or 3:00 p.m. at the very latest. To my surprise when 10:00 pm came and there was still no sign of Audie, I became anxious to say the least. One of the many things that I hated about Audie's new job was that he could not have a cell phone on him, which meant absolutely no contact at all once he left home. And he didn't get breaks and lunches, which caused more alarm for me about him. I worried about him all the time and prayed for him continuously.

On that particular night, I noticed that there was something that was just off. I was restless and could not shake the mood no matter what. Audie was relentlessly on my mind. I felt compelled to pray for him. I grabbed my cell phone and tried at least five to six different times to contact him but to no avail. His phone kept going to voicemail. That worried me even the more because by now, it was way pass the legal time for him to be off work and at home.

Somewhere in the midst of it all, I must have dozed off because I suddenly felt a nudge that warned me to get up and pray for Audie. I knew the voice of God, and I knew that the Spirit was telling me, almost commanding me, to pray fervently and to do it immediately! Not just pray but to pray specifically about him, over him, and for him that he was in spiritual danger and warfare that the enemy was after his life.

With that warning, I didn't even blink or think twice, I rolled out the bed, hit the floor, grabbed the phone, and immediately texted my niece Lisa in Atlanta and asked her to pray with me over Audie. I was visibly upset and shaken by the spiritual news I had just received. Even though I was shaken I was very thankful that God would think so much of me to provide me with a warning before the enemy had time to strike.

I praised God for that. Lisa and I prayed together. We pulled down strongholds until we were 100 percent assured that the stronghold(s) had exposed and broken. We knew that the devil was not only a liar, he was very much so defeated and God had given my family and my household total victory! As I continued to pray alone, I eventually heard the garage door go up, and it was my baby coming in. I could hear him downstairs, and after a while, he got something to eat and came upstairs. He looked so weary, worn, and tired.

We talked for a minute, and then I went back to sleep. The next morning, I didn't wake him because I knew that he was extremely tired and worn out from the day before. I had to leave the house at 4:30 a.m. to start my first shift of work at the hotel. I kissed Audie on the forehead and said, "Bye, baby, have a good day. I'll call you later." With that, I left for work. Concerned and still praying I knew that all wasn't quite over yet, but God!

Later that day, he called me on his way to work. They had actually called him in on an early shift because someone else did not show up again. Tired and worn out, but still trying to do the noble thing, he went in. He should have quite and never went back in my opinion. I hated that job for him and didn't have too much respect for those that held office over him there because they didn't have a good system put in place for their employees.

They seemingly didn't care about their employee's well-being or their family time. All they cared about was an employee working themselves to the bone. By Monday afternoon, Audie could barely keep his eyes open. He was so sleepy and just beat down. We talked, and I urged him to give notice and never look back.

I told him that he was my priority and that he could quit today for all I cared and we would be fine. God would continue to provide for us and that he didn't need to work so hard and such ungodly, unscrupulous hours. His health was the absolute most important thing to me. Nothing else about that job mattered to me the most.

On Tuesday, Audie went back to work. This time, he felt overwhelmingly sluggish, unable to keep his balance, his breathing became laborious, even his vision was questionable while on his route. He reached out to his employers on more than one, two, three, or maybe even four occasions, practically begging to end the route and come in early and was repeatedly denied access to do so.

When he obviously could no longer function, he was told in an unprofessional, disrespectful manner to return the bus only to find out that his supervisor had been monitoring him and his driving behavior all along and never bothered to chime in or stop the bus and check on him even though he repeatedly told them that at the moment he was not doing well.

Eventually the so-called supervisor approached him and once again, in my opinion, cared more about the bus route than a human being's life. He ordered my husband to take the bus back to the barn and meet him in the human resources department, and Audie complied.

Automatically, he was met again by unfriendly, unprofessional, and uncompassionate people who called themselves supervisors and managers. I would not even treat my pet the way Audie was treated that day all because of the makeshift power and the almighty dollar that he wasn't making on a job that didn't really pay all that much to begin with.

They did everything but throw him out. They wrote him up, criticized his work, and basically were getting ready to fire him at this point. With all the energy and strength Audie had in his body, he took of his badge, gave them some other documentation, and said, "That's enough." And he was done.

I thank God for Jesus that I was not aware of this or any of this action prior to when I got off work or the story could have been much differently. I have a kind, gentle, humble husband whose sole purpose in life is to live for Christ, be a covering for his family, and serve the Lord with all his heart. Anyone that knows him knows his demeanor is extremely humbling. It takes an act of Congress for him to give up, quit, or get angry—all in that same order.

I am not saying that he is perfect. However, he does know how to treat others, and it is always genuine. When I got home and he was telling me the story, he had to sit on me to keep me from going back downtown. I thought how someone dared to speak to him in such an uncaring, unprofessional, hateful manner. I was perturbed to say the least and wanted to tell those individuals that they may not like Audie or care for him, but they will respect the person that he is; after all, those individuals were someone's employee as well and just like Audie could be fired as easily as he. I wasn't having it at all. That night, I think I probably averaged a minimal five hours of sleep if that much.

That Wednesday, Audie stayed home. I begged him to get some rest. He promised me that he would. One of his many passions is to cook and that he did well. So by the time I got home, he had already cooked dinner, took the dog for a long walk, and was just waiting for me.

The next day we had talked, texted a couple of times during the day, and I couldn't wait to get home to him. For some strange reason around 3:00 p.m. on September 18, I tried calling him on his cell phone, and it went straight to voicemail. I didn't leave a message, and I decided that I would call back later.

Around 3:15 p.m. once again, I felt the same uneasy feeling. Only this time it was more heightened. So I called both the house and cell phone, but both were met with his unanswered voice, just the voice message. It was at this point that I really began to worry because not being able to get in touch with him was not his forte.

When the clock turned to 4:30 p.m. and I still had not heard from him via any communication, I panicked. I knew that I needed to get home right away. I prayed all the way home and tried to remain calm. I asked God to please watch over and protect my home from any danger. It's my habit to enter through garage door. However this time, I came in the garage door and headed to the office, calling his name repeatedly. There was no response. Although I saw his truck in the garage, he was nowhere in sight. I called his name again, still no response.

FROM WIFE MODE INTO SERVANTHOOD

After entering our home cautiously, I heard a really light, faint noise. I stopped dead in my tracks and just listened. That's when I heard him say, "I'm okay, baby, I just fell. Don't worry, I'm fine." The problem with that statement was he kept repeating the cycle over and over again to the point of it sounding robotic.

I knew the sound was coming from the office and prepared myself mentally for the worst. As I walked around the corner into the office, I no sooner took three steps. There I saw him lying on the floor in almost fetal position, reaching out to me, and saying not to worry about him, that he was going to be fine. I screamed his name asked God to help us. I picked up the phone and immediately called 911.

They were there within minutes. When they entered the house, they asked questions and began to prepare to take him away. One of the paramedics came back into the house and said, "Ma'am, is it okay if I prayed with you?" Even though I was in pain and distraught by what I had just witnessed, I was moved at the same time with his compassion to pray for us as well. "Of course you can," was my reply to him. He held my hands and right in our hallway, we both bowed our heads, and he prayed for our household and specifically for Audie.

Everything was quiet. I felt the powerful almighty calmness of God entering in. I sat down in the formal dining room and just cried. The next thing I noticed was seeing the feet of several people in my home, and they were praying fervently in Spanish. I knew they were praying for me and Audie because every now and then I could hear his name being mentioned.

When I looked up, this little boy spoke to me, and he said, "Ma'am, don't worry. Your husband is going to be alright. God is going to take care of him." I just looked at him; my heart ached in pain like never before. All I could do at that point was smile. There were no words to utter, and all I could think of was but God!

I called my next-door neighbor, Pat, who had been a very good friend to us. She immediately came running, and we both hugged and cried. She adored Audie and him likewise with her. The tears my neighbor shed were heartfelt and genuine. The neighbor hugged me close and kept saying, "Brenda, God is able." I was numb. All I could think about was, "Now, God, what will you have me do in this instance? Where do I go from this moment, you must lead me because I don't know the way."

As I looked around the house, I could put together remnants of what Audie's day must have been like. For instance, I saw both the patio doors opened and that he had done some cleaning on the patios and the back porch. There were garbage bags displayed about the house. He must have been gathering up trash for Friday's pickup.

His running shoes, headset, and other workout materials was beside him on the floor. In the kitchen, he had taken out food to cook. The television was still on where he had been watching a movie, and the movie was now over, and the television still reflected "On Demand." The computer was still on and displayed the last e-mail he had sent to me.

The phone in the kitchen displayed several missed message that were all from me. After the emergency medical services left the house, I stayed for a while and prayed, "Lord, please strengthened me for this journey. I need you now more than ever." I needed his permission to move forward from that point forward.

After making sure that the house was secured, me and my two neighbors left for the hospital. Upon arrival there, we were told that Audie was in the emergency room being prepped for ICU. He had indeed suffered a stroke. Within twenty-four hours, he had swelling on the left side of his brain, paralyzed on his left side. A tumor was also developing on his left side, and he was experiencing seizures. He was admitted into ICU with very limited visitation. I called people I knew who loved us and would pray on our behalf, and they answered and came to the hospital.

The genuine love we received at the outset was overwhelming to say the least. Both our neighbors stayed with me until three a.m., the next morning and then the neighbor brought us back home.

I went to bed for about an hour and then got dressed for work at four and went to both jobs; if anyone asked me how that happened, I would have to respond, by the sheer grace and unmerited mercy of my Lord and Savior Jesus Christ. After getting to work, I informed my bosses of what had taken place they both asked me why I bothered to come in to work when such a tragedy had taken place.

My response was that bills still needed to be paid, and all we had were each other to lean and depend upon earthly speaking. Honestly, I did not have any other choice. I knew that God was with me, but God also give his people wisdom in the process of how to go about life and that isn't putting your head in the sand and pretending everything is fine.

From that moment forward, the days and the tasks before me became relentless. Dealing with the hospitals and nurses, advocates, nursing home attendants, rehabilitation centers were ruthless; and while not all of them were considered as unprofessional, the bulk of them were.

Audie remained in Harris Methodist Hospital for three consecutive months, and I stayed each and every night with him while I continued to work both jobs. So typically, my days would begin as early as 3:00 a.m. and would not end until around 1:30 a.m. the next day. His needs were just that great, and I wanted to make sure that he knew he was not alone in the fight for his life.

Daily I would visit my husband on my breaks and lunch. I stayed overnight. I washed his face, combed his hair, monitored his medicine, read to him, talked to him, prayed over him, watched over him, held his hand, and told him that it would be alright. There were many days the pain for him was unbearable and the situation looked bleak. His vision was challenged. His speech at times was slurred, and he was unable to eat for at least one week.

But he never lost hope. He has a fight in him that is tenacious. There were many phone calls and texts that poured in, inquiring about how he looked. Was his speech impaired? Was his face contorted? Was he paralyzed all over? How was he really doing? Keep us in the loop. Why aren't you calling and telling us what is really going on?

People were angry with me and challenging me across the board. Some perhaps were questioning whether or not I even knew what I was doing, as it relates to his care or medical needs being met. All that I knew in that moment was that God was on our side, and he was the only one that I was concerned with. I could not and would not allow any outside forces to cause me to go in any other direction because too many important factors and lives depended upon faith and belief.

While Audie was in Harris Hospital, the woman who was supposed to be his advocate acted as anything but. She was mean-spirited. She was angry with us just for questioning some things at all. She never let me live it down that I worked two part-time jobs, even telling me point blank, "Just how are you supposed to take care of him when you work two part-time jobs? At best, he will need to go to a nursing home after he leaves here because you will not be able to take care of him at home." Day after day, I endured her relentless torturing and endless insults. Three weeks of Audie being in Harris Hospital came the phone calls and barrage of questioning regarding insurance and who was responsible for the bill and the next phase of care.

After just the first week of Audie being in the hospital, he received a letter from the company where he was employed that his insurance with United Health Care had been terminated immediately and that he had thirty days to contact COBRA if he was interested in securing coverage from elsewhere. Not only that. I also received a bill from the EMS of $1,635.00 for their services, and this amount was due NOW!

My response was, "But God!" It gets better. Days after that, the medical bills started to pile up, and the phone calls came in one right after the other. The advocate was making decisions about Audie's next level of care behind my back and talking to him about what his alternatives would be. They would tell him after I left for work that he would have to be moved to a nursing home. Thank you, Jesus, God said not so!

By the time I would come back to check on Audie between jobs, often exhausted and downtrodden from dealing with the enemy on every hand, I would find countless of pamphlets with forced scribbled signatures from my husband that could not at the time rationally make decisions for himself; despite my pleading with all hospital personnel to contact me directly where Audie's overall health was concerned being totally ignored.

I would leave all points of contact information such as home, cell, work, and e-mail addresses—not one person respected my wishes. They simply did whatever they wanted to do, and they continued to disrespect both our wishes on the phone and in person.

There would be many days they would scream, yell, and simply reminded me that I was just a part-timer with limited income and no medical experience to take care of Audie in his endless recovery. At my very low point, I will admit I cried and felt temporarily helpless. I don't regret it, because that particular cry provided strength, clarity, wisdom, hope, joy, and peace in the process of moving forward. It reminded me that I was human and that the task was tremendous, but it also reminded me that Jehovah was indeed on my side and that he found me worthy to handle the task at hand.

I remembered having an old Kleenex tissue box in the car with me that still had a few unused Kleenex in the bottom of it. I came to myself and grabbed that box and I looked in the mirror. What I saw was a woman saddened, wounded, hurt, tired, over-worked and underpaid, sleep deprived, overwhelmed, scared, and frightened. But God! I found myself wondering how in the world could I feel so alone in a world with countless of other people yet felt like I was by myself left to deal with a situation that was totally out of my control and comfort zone.

After taking a long hard look at that woman glancing back at me in that mirror, I decided right then and there that I was going to TRUST God in the midst of it all. "God," I said, "if this is the hand that I have been dealt, I am not asking for you to please give me the strength to make it happen. I am asking for you to become my mighty fortress, strength, source, resources, compass, healer, provider, protector, friend, covering, refuge, lamp, and counsel because where I am now I am going to need absolutely nothing less than all of that and more and I know you to be unlimited in all of the above."

I made up my mind right then and there to say goodbye to the old me and hello to the new woman on the horizon. I did not know exactly how God was going to bring us out, but one thing that I never ever doubted about it was if he brought us to it, he was surely going to bring us through it. One night I called my next door and asked her if she could use some company for a while. She was quick to say, "Yes, please come right over."

I never regretted a moment of our time together. This woman took me in under her wings, and for the next seven to eight nights, she watched over me and cared for me like a mother hen. She was up at 3:45 a.m., cooking me breakfast (pancakes and syrup), grits, and coffee. No request was denied. She would call me in the evenings and ask me when I would be coming home and wait for me to come home and wash up so that we could eat together.

When I tried to repay her, she absolutely refused. Upon thanking her for her time, care, compassion, and hospitality, Pat would often say to me, with tears in her eyes, "Brenda, you don't know what you and Audie has done for me over the years. I truly love you both, and this I want to do."

Sadly, after these precious days with Pat, and I returned home, I only got to see her for a short time afterwards because she was moving away with her only son in St. Louis, Illinois. When I found out that she was leaving and moving away, we hugged and cried endlessly because we both understood that this would be our last time seeing each other—not only in Fort Worth but period.

Pat discovered that she had dementia, and she was having trouble remembering things. This was a scary and terrible time in her life and the rest of us. To this day, I miss her friendship terribly and pray and think of her often. I really miss her friend and would give almost anything to have her back in my life, but God knew that at that particular moment, what we shared was priceless.

In October 2012, Audie was eventually moved to the HealthSouth Rehabilitation Center off Lancaster Avenue after fighting tooth and nail with the insurance company, hospital administrators, nurses, and virtually everyone else involved. I was exhausted but never lost my focus. I continually prayed and fasted for weeks on end. "Your Grace Is Amazing" was my truth and song.

One day, after I saw that I was getting nowhere with the hospital when Audie needed to be moved to another facility, the Holy Spirit lead me to contact the hospital charity department. I asked if they could help me in getting him moved due to a lapse in his insurance coverage.

The woman was very nice—one of the first up until this point. She asked me general information and said that she would be sending me out an application and requested that I complete it and forward it back to her within ten business days. I completed the application and did as she requested. After not hearing anything from her, I contacted the department once again and attempted to speak with who was supposed to be our advocate. Truly she was anything but. She was adamant about not receiving any type of insurance check and until that happened, she stated that Audie would not be moving anywhere!

Finally, I became annoyed with her ranting, raving, and screaming in my ear. So I asked "What are you talking about, what check, and who is it supposed to come from?" Come to find out, over two weeks ago, the hospital had graciously agreed to pay for a month of Audie's rehabilitation, and she, the supposedly advocate, had not even mentioned this at all! Nor was she trying to assist me in the process. Because of her arrogances and mean ways, Audie missed two weeks of necessary rehabilitation that costs the both of us not only more money but precious time together in the healing process! This was another blow to what was setup to be a setback for Audie's rehabilitation…but God!

The more this evil person fought Audie being transferred, the more I continued in prayer. I normally would come home on Wednesday nights to gather the mail, wash clothes, and get another set of clothing for the remainder of the week. It was dark, cold, and scary outside as I entered the house and was walking into their living room I heard the Holy Spirit say, "And I make my sheep to lie down in green pastures." This was crystal clear to me. I stopped dead in my tracks. I wasn't scared because I knew the voice his voice of the Holy Spirit, but I was curious as to what it meant; particularly, what he was saying to me in this hour.

Needless to say, I continued the task at hand. I put the clothes in the washer, gathered the mail, fed the dog, and made me a sandwich. Then I got in the middle of my bed and started going through the mail. Once again, there it was. This still, direct, and matter-of-fact voice, saying, "And I make my sheep to lie down in green pastures." This time I completely stopped what I was doing and devoted all my time and attention to the matter at hand. I calmed my spirit and asked God to please speak to me so that I would understand his precepts. When I did, this is the response that I received.

I was given the wisdom to know that in the twenty-third book of Psalms, when David was asked to lead the sheep from the valley up to the mountaintop, the journey didn't happen without trials, challenges, and difficulties. Quite the contrary, David was tested, tried, weary, and challenged. According to 101 Info, sheep by nature have a strong instinct to follow the sheep in front of them. When one sheep decides to go somewhere, the rest of the flock usually follows, even if it is not a good decision.

For example, sheep will follow each other to slaughter. If one sheep jumps over a cliff, the others are likely to follow. Even from birth, lambs are conditioned to follow the older members of the flock. This instinct is hardwired into sheep. It's not something they "think" about.

This is a frightening truth at best. Nevertheless, David was given this incredible task to lead the sheep. In David's efforts to do so, he had to depend upon God to see this particular task through successfully. If he was to make it to his final destination weary or not, he must remain focused. No doubt for David, at times during this journey, it must have appeared to him to become cumbersome, overwhelming, and stressful. But he remained faithful to the task assigned. In the days ahead of David's journey, perhaps his number one focus was on the end result—getting to the mountain top safely and assuredly with the sheep.

Because of his timing in reaching the assigned destination, and perhaps the setbacks and delays due to unscheduled events during the journey, he discovered the grass was much higher than expected upon reaching the mountaintop. It appeared differently due to the high volume of grass that had grown.

David is asked to make the sheep to "lie down in the green pastures." Ordinarily, sheep are not known to lie down, especially completely out on the ground; and now, here they are being ordered to do so.

In David's case, after the sheep were lying still on the ground under the tall grass, when the enemy showed up, they thought that nothing or no one was there because they were used to climbing the mountaintop and taking out the sheep with little or no effort, because typically the sheep are all standing there, totally unaware of the danger that is present, and therefore, made easy prey for their enemy.

Through the revelation of God, I was instantly instilled with the knowledge that I too was to go to bed and lie down and be still (rest in the Lord) in the midst of all that I personally had going on. God had me covered, and he was never letting me go.

The Word of the Lord came so strongly in saying, "Brenda, like Isaiah 43:2, New International Version (NIV) says, "When you (Brenda), pass through the waters, I will be with you; and when you (Brenda) pass through the rivers, they will not sweep over you.

When you (Brenda) walk through the fire, you (Brenda) will not be burned; the flames will not set you ablaze." Praise God, praise God, and praise God!

Not only did I sleep well that night, but I continued to do so afterwards. In fact, each day, I could readily tell and feel the inner strength within my being become more strengthened. I knew beyond a shadow of a doubt that God was with me. I could sense and feel his presence at all times.

When I continued to go before counsel, I was no longer afraid of what to say, how to interact among them, or what the situation may have appeared to be for that matter. I had God on my side, and he was fighting my every battle and being armed with that knowledge and assurance. I knew that I had his victory. Praise God.

As it turns out, due to an error on the advocate's part, the hospital paid for two months of Audie's rehabilitation therapy. Now came the fight of getting him into a reputable place for continual healing. The current hospital he was in became adamant about placing him in a skilled nursing home, and my response was always no because I wasn't sending my precious covering off to some tiny room with no windows, looking at a wall and chanting all day. Audie is enameled with life from the Lord and dying or recessing was not an option nor was it even a strong suggestion from my standpoint. The devil and his entire army was a LIAR!

NOW, FAITH IS!

One day, as I was heading out into the cold for my morning break, I began praying and asking God to show me the next move because I wanted to make sure that I was continuing to flow in his expressed divine will. I didn't have room for errors and hypotheticals; I needed truth that is God's truth and realities.

God lead me to contact one of the members from my current church and inquire about a suitable rehabilitation center. As it turned out, he was the exact person that I needed for that exact hour. He answered the phone and was excited to hear from me. I told him what I needed, and he said, "Yes, Audie can come here to our facility to recover. We would be glad to have him here." Thank you Lord!

When I reported this information back to the hospital, they referred me to a woman by the name of Pam to contact her directly about their facility. At first, the woman appeared to be all sweet, professional, and very compassionate about our situation. However, after she hung up from speaking to me, the woman went over to the hospital and spoke with Audie's advocate and immediately changed her way of thinking and backtracked all of her previous conversations with me.

Well, the advocate called me livid, shouting on the phone that Audie was not a good candidate. She added that this particular rehabilitation did not want to accept him because he was not strong enough to pass the required testing and their suggestion for a skilled nursing facility still stand.

At that point, I contacted the original rehabilitation and asked them personally if they would receive Audie. They did not only say yes, they went the distance to make it happen. I simply thanked God quietly. In fact, their CEO went to the hospital and did the preliminary testing and paperwork to accept Audie into their facility and received him in their facility before the week was over.

By Tuesday, Audie was in his new facility and received the royal treatment upon move in! A special dinner was planned for the both us upon entry, and the rehabilitation center also had arranged for a private room for me to stay with him if I choose to…but God!

I stayed with him at every available moment that I could. I was there for his breakfast, therapy sessions, and lunch until he closed his eyes at night to sleep. He is my best friend, my covering, and my heart—there was no place else I wanted to be but with him no matter what we were facing. As the days went forth, I watched as God continued to provide healing and refuge for Audie's journey.

There were days when the therapy became seemingly unbearable, and he would pass out or sleep for hours upon hours afterwards. No matter what, we kept praying and agreeing that he was healed and that God's Word would prevail. Each day I left Audie for work, I declared that he should live and not die! We would pray together and believe that God was indeed with us.

One weekend, I stayed at the rehabilitation center with Audie but ran home for a few minutes to check on things. Upon returning, Audie said to me, "Gaines came by to see me." I thought, Gaines came by to see you, how was that possible he didn't even know you were here. So I dismissed the thought of him being there because I didn't think anyone knew. A few minutes later, the nurse came in and she said, "Whew, I would have never made it with his shower this morning had it not been for that nice young man who came and helped me." Audie looked up at and said, "I told ya he came."

I was too outdone and just gave a sheepish smile and put my head down. Audie told me that Deacon Gaines had actually showed up, got in the shower with him, and helped him before going back home and going to church. I called him when I got home and tried to thank him, but the words turned into thankful tears down my face.

He said, "I know, I know, sister. I'm here for the both of you." To God be all the glory that is rightfully due his name. Audie continued to receive visitors throughout the weeks. The facility had good nurses and horrible nurses. We experienced good days and challenging days, but that is all a part of life's journey.

Eventually the time came for Audie to leave the rehab and go into the next phase of his healing process, warranting another major decision-making goal. During this time, I was seeking the Lord for answers and directions. The Lord led me to bring him home for care. As eager and excited as I was, the task set before me seemed gigantic at best. For starters, I couldn't physically see how this was going to happen.

I had no home health experience and exposure, let alone expertise. I had to work for a living to keep a roof over our heads and food on the table. I was working two jobs that required me to get up at 3:00 a.m. and return home, if I was fortunate, at 7:00 p.m., and maybe to bed by 10:30 p.m. then back up and at it the same time the next day. But I continued to seek the will of God for my next level.

In the following weeks to come, I felt the presence and peace of God to continue to move forward with bringing Audie home. No further instructions were given at that time. So I set my face and my desire to do so. The next several weeks were plagued with people from my employment to various naysayers asking about Audie's status: Can he talk, walk, and eat? What does his face look like? Is he paralyzed? How are you going to take care of him? Don't you work two different jobs?

Can you afford help to come in and assist you with him? I immediately said no to all of the above, but God can. And he will and he has. You see, by the time the devil finds it out, my God will have already worked it out.

Mind you, not any of these individuals cared, knew, or were really concerned about our "true" needs at all. At best, they were people taking a break from their own personal issues, trying to find some sense of solace, break, or relief in their situation for the moment. Most of these people didn't have a true desire to see my family prosper or overcome this temporary trial.

They were busy telling me what had happened to people "they knew" who had a same or similar problem or individuals, who simply never recovered from their problems. And when I refused to take any part of their conversations, or thought process, I was looked upon as being in some form of denial. My only stance at that moment was what does God have to say about my situation and whose report do I really believe.

On one particular morning during my first shift, the store was extremely busy with customers and all hands were on deck. I was at the cash register and working the RTD case and anything else that needed my general attention, when my boss blurted out in no professional fashion, "Heah, Brenda! So, what's the deal with your husband? I mean is he paralyzed or what? I mean just how bad is it really? Will he ever be able to walk again? He isn't that old is he? Poor thing, I don't know if he will be able to come back from something this bad. It appears that he is in pretty bad shape, and you having to work two different jobs and all, poor thing, I don't how in the world you do it."

I looked at him and said, "He may not be at his best right this moment, but he is much better off than you right now and I kept it moving." What the enemy didn't know was I usually fight my best warfare when my back is against the wall and I don't have a whole lot of options to choose from. My fight was not with people silly or otherwise. It wasn't even about me and my spouse.

It was about the life lessons learned, the wisdom I had attained through immediate obedience, and the level of faith that we both had to learn how to work in moments of seemingly despair and defeat, stress degradation, embarrassment and hardship.

I cared more about trusting and depending upon God than wondering what everybody else thought of me. I no longer worried about what I was going to eat for dinner that night, or the everyday mundane things that only come to self-serve the human psyche; instead, I chose to set my mind on Christ and look to him for all the answers that I needed. If he didn't direct me in a particular manner, then I didn't move until otherwise. Daily, my prayer was "God, all I need is a word from you and until that happens, I am standing on the last thing that you said."

When this frame of mind set in, I saw daily transformation being manifested in my life. Instantly I witnessed inner strength, supernatural changes that cannot be explained taking place right before my very eyes. Daily I experienced a true peace that outweighed my natural understanding. While standing eye-level with trouble on every leaning side, being exposed to pain in my body, weariness and a stress level like I had never experienced before, I no longer doubted God's presence with me because it was apparent at each moment.

I was constantly in remembrance that the God I dialogued with daily in private was deliberately unveiling Himself to me publically. I knew that the one I preached about, praised too, cried out too in the middle of the night was holding me and sheltering me from EVERY vicious storm.

Daily the Lord was comforting me, wiping away my tears, keeping me from falling, upholding me with his right hand. I knew for sure He was forever holding back the night for me. Making my enemies behave. Opening and shutting doors, making ways out of no way. Daily He was taking me and my family from glory to glory. When I got that revelation down in my spirit, I knew that I was safe in the master's arms and I was now being "fitted" for his expressed use only! Absolutely nothing else truly mattered.

It no longer mattered to me who came to see about us who even cared about us, lying, back-biting, wished ill thoughts on us. Nothing mattered because I realized that the greater was already present, and he wasn't going anywhere. Daily, weekly, hourly, and finally minute by minute I found myself consistently being thankful and grateful. I would worship whenever and wherever it was possible—at work, in the car, in the rehab, during therapy, in the office—it just didn't matter. All I knew was that all was well because God got me and I am glad about it.

Though the rehab fought me tooth and nail about my final decision regarding Audie, I had the final say and I brought him home with no true agenda or plan already being laid out. All I had was my word from God, and that to me was enough!

PHASE 2: COMING HOME

"So you will find favor and good repute
in the sight of God and man. Trust in the Lord with all
your heart and do not lean on your own understanding.
In all your ways acknowledge Him, And He will make
your paths straight."

—Proverbs 3:4–5

I remember very vividly walking into Audie's room to tell him the good news about bringing him home. Prior to that day, he would ask me, "Heah, babe, are you here to bust me out? I really want to go home." At that time, he was just not strong enough to do so, and he required a lot of attention and assistance. For me, it was imperative that I worked to keep a roof over our heads so that when he was released, he would actually have a place to call home again.

That evening after work, I walked into Audie's room. He was looking out of the window, and as I was getting ready to say something to him, the Holy Spirit spoke and said, "Don't say anything just watch him." As I stood in the doorway and watched Audie, I could see this faraway look on his face that appeared to be asking the question, "How much longer will I be here?" Tears rolled down my face, and I knew I must move forward no matter what to find a better solution for my beloved.

December 1, 2012 was Audie's go home date. He was so excited. The week leading up to his departure, I said to him, "Heah, babe, the time has come for me to bust you out." At first, he looked at me, just staring without words. Finally when he could speak, with tears rolling down his face, he said, "Really, babe, I am finally going to get to go home? How are you going to be able to take care of me?

Everyone here is saying that you won't be able to do it?" I smiled and said, "They are absolutely correct, I won't be, but God will. You see when he gives a direct order; he alone has already made the necessary provisions to make it happen.

Audie smiled, and we both just rejoiced in that solace that God was good and able. As a last-minute trick from the enemy, there was this particular company out from Irving, Texas, called and wanted to send Audie some brochures and pamphlets about their facility. They swore it would be a blessing to Audie in continuing his at home rehab.

The gentleman invited me out to do a tour of their facility, and I asked a girlfriend of mines to attend with me. I took off time from work to go out and make a site visit. The site visit turned out to be a two and a half hour visit, which included the gentleman showing us the entire facility along with their outpatient gymnasium where Audie would be completing his weekly rehab. We talked at great lengths about the challenges that Audie would be facing both now and in the future. We also discussed potential assistance that he would need and the best methods for those needs while attending this state–of-the art facility.

The gentleman did a follow-up call after our meeting and explained that he had already spoken with my insurance company and gotten a verbal approval for Audie to be accepted into this program and appeared to be excited about him attending. I counted at least seven to ten times during our meeting both in person and on the phone that I specifically stated to this person that Audie would only be attending their facility as an outpatient. He swore he understood, and once again, pretended to be all in.

Audie came home on Friday, November 30. We celebrated our twenty-seventh wedding anniversary while in the rehab, which was okay. We celebrated together, and that was all that mattered to the both of us. I remember when I went to pick Audie up after work on that Friday; the doctor had not signed the release paperwork and was off the floor, taking care of another patient. The staff nurse acted as though she didn't know what was going on. She said Audie had not been scheduled to leave the facility according to her records.

It didn't matter whether she had understanding in the issue or not. It was the divine date prescheduled for Audie's release, and release was the operative word used and abided by. I asked for the doctor. So the release was signed, little did I know that a friend of the family, Deacon Gaines had already packed up Audie's things. The only thing left for me to do was make our grand exit, and that's what we did. We were humbled and thankful, but ready to move forward to the next divine chapter in our lives.

When we got home, people were already parked in front of our house. Cars were pulling up, furniture was being delivered, and this particular person who showed up during the last two weeks of Audie's rehab was in the crowd. It reminded me of a particular scripture: "Now there was a day when the sons of God came to present themselves before the Lord, and Satan also came among them" (Job 1:6, ASV). There was this strange woman who would periodically come to Audie's room when I was not around.

Apparently she would whisper to him that she would love to be able to assist him with his rehab once Audie was released. She continued to tell him that she worshipped at the same church as we did. She stated, "You know my folks. My uncle is one of the preachers there," and even offered us her mom's cell phone number to call as a personal reference. After all, she was a "Christian."

As Audie kept mentioning her name to me, I pretty much took it in stride, not really giving much care or concern to her request. However, on the last week that he was in rehab, she appeared out of nowhere and formally introduced herself to me, stating the same things she had already told Audie. I asked a series of questions until I felt somewhat comfortable. I called the reference, and of course her mother sung her praises as if she was the greatest invention since sliced bread. She ended the conversation by saying, "She would be a tremendous blessing to both you and Deacon Murphy."

On Monday morning of December 3, 2012, Audie was supposed to be picked up by this company in Dallas for rehab until 2:00 p.m. He was supposed to have speech, occupational, and physical therapy. He was also supposed to have lunch and return home by 3:00 p.m. To my surprise, none of this happened as mentioned during my series of multiple conversations at the facility. The facility sent this skinny little scrawny girl who had just gotten back from vacation and possessed a hateful, unprofessional, and careless attitude. She came in the door raising hell.

She drove up in an SUV weighing 108 pounds, that's including her shoes being on. Luckily, Deacon Gaines was at our home when she showed up ill prepared as she tried to bring Audie out of the front door face forward with the wheelchair. Had it not been for the sheer grace and mercy of God and for the quick wit and knee jerk reaction of Deacon Gaines, Audie would have simply slid out the chair face forward onto the concrete and could have suffered a severe setback.

Should that have happened, I most likely would be writing this book from a totally different perspective with a title that would have read From the Inside Out. All I could say at the time was, "Thank God for Jesus!" I called at least four to five times that day to the facility, trying to find out the whereabouts of my husband and how he was doing.

The original person that I spoke with finally had the spine to pick up the phone and say something like, "Oh, bless his heart. Audie has had quite a day. He will be a little tired when he gets home, but he should be okay." When I asked what that meant, he chose not to further elaborate. Now, I was extremely worried about what he meant. I could not wait to get home to see for myself. Upon arriving home, Deacon Gaines informed me what had actually taken place.

He said that from the very beginning, the facility was late in picking Audie up. The woman, or should I say child that picked him up did not want to be there. She was arrogant, lazy, and uncaring. Audie said that once Deacon Gaines assisted him into the SUV. He was at a point where he could not keep his balance enough to sit up straight without assistance. It didn't matter to her. She just jumped in and took off. On the way, she muttered something like, "This makes me sick. You're just dead weight to me."

Armed with this devastating information, I took the next twenty-four hours off before I called that facility and prayed for them first and then myself for self-control. When I called, I asked to speak with the director of the facility, who I was told was out for the day but would return my call. When she did, she had concerns as to why Audie did not show up the next day.

I told the director of the treatment or the lack thereof, that Audie had received on Monday. At first she tried to appear shocked and surprised. The first thing out of her mouth was, "Who did this? I want their name." I asked the nurse if she had checked his file, how many people could have been assigned to him; yet no one was looking out for Audie's well-being at all.

Later that night, we talked about his experience at the facility and what he told me broke my heart into pieces. Audie said, "Bren, the person you had been dealing with counseled me for two to four hours nonstop about signing papers to live on the campus and not return home to Fort Worth. He kept saying that by signing those papers, I would be doing my wife a favor because she cannot afford to take care of you any longer."

This cold-hearted lack of a human being had the audacity to say to Audie: "I mean. C'mon she is working two part-time jobs, trying to take care of you. I mean, do you really want her to go through all of this by herself?" No one other than Satan himself would have uttered such words. Thank you, Jesus, Audie knew the voice of his redeemer. He knew that I loved him and that there was nothing that I would not do for him within my power.

Thankfully, even being in the presence of sheer evil, he still had enough presence of mind to believe God for the truth to be revealed. I tried mightily to keep him out of the loop of worry, frustration, and warfare; however, sometimes it just could not be avoided.

Daily, I witnessed firsthand the ruthlessness of some of the hospital caretakers; there were rehabilitation staff who took full advantage of patients' limitations. Often I would return to Audie's room to find unwanted brochures trying to force Audie to make a choice between returning home and signing forms that he clearly did not understand to admit him into a nursing facility of some type.

On one occasion, I was told by Audie about how he felt forced after relentless torturing of guilt by an agency to sign his name the best he could on the paperwork in an attempt to stay at a nursing facility for 60 days due to the agent telling him that he was in my way. But thank God for grace and mercy, the original paperwork came home with Audie in his pocket, as opposed to remaining at the facility as the enemy had planned.

After dealing with the facility and telling them what I thought of their state-of-the-art world-renown building and staff, I strongly suggested that they never contact me again or they would be hearing from my attorneys. What kinds of people don't have a heart, yet they still are able to prey on others while giving the appearance of being human? From that point, I stop operating in the "wife" mode and endeavored to operate only in the "servant" mode. This caused me to function in a whole differ-ent capacity to flow and to accomplish the task at hand.

After Audie came home, I felt that I had no other option but to give this woman from the rehab a try to assist us. From the beginning I explained to her that we were not in any position to pay her a full-time, part-time, or contingency salary, but we would from time to time give her funds as the Lord provided. She knew that going into the arrangement, there was never any hidden agenda from my side; and the woman or shyster readily agreed. At the time, I needed the assistance of others.

Against everything in me, I accepted this woman into our home and into our private lives. In the beginning, this woman would come over and assist with whatever needed to be done. Right off the bat, she wanted to make necessary changes as she saw fit such as having ramps put up out front, have the doors removed, and went as far as to speak to various agencies behind my back regarding the same. I asked her to stop with the cleaning, washing, and definitely cooking. It took all the resolve in me to have this woman in my house around my husband and into our private world, especially when I was not home.

That for me was when the stretching truly began. I prayed to God constantly. I fasted and I cried out to him with all of my being: "Lord, this is costing me everything that I am and what I know to be true within myself. I have to depend upon you for total guidance and direction. Please speak, Lord. Your servant Brenda is listening."

Being very familiar with this scriptural reference, I began to read and meditate upon 2 Corinthians 4:8–10 (ESV): "We are afflicted in every way, but not crushed; perplexed, but not despairing; persecuted, but not forsaken; struck down, but not destroyed; always carrying about in the body the dying of Jesus, so that the life of Jesus also may be manifested in our bodies."

Day and night going and coming, I would say this over and over until it became my personal mantra. At this point, no one else's voice could soothe me. I felt that the old me I once knew had vacated the premises, and I was not sure if she would ever be returning. This new woman that was on the scene was more assured, becoming more affirmed in her daily walk and faith in Christ.

She was becoming fortified in every sense of the word, and what I realized the most was that if I were going to survive this warfare, I must become cognizant of the fact of the battle that I was in and where its battleground relies. I knew in my heart it's time to get suited up for the game and make another move without my warfare clothes intact.

Without a shadow of a doubt, I knew I was being pulled mentally into several areas. I was challenged on every hand daily. I was being talked to any kind of way, people were scamming left and right, money was tight, so-called friends were extremely few, family was not around, and the wolves came out in droves for the constant kill.

Daily, I was asked—via texts, e-mails, phone calls—"Are you still living at your old address? Do you still have your cars? How is Audie today? I heard this and that." The devil had set his sights on wiping us out, and he was attempting to do so through the use of my mind, curt words, evil intentions, setups, disappointments, setbacks, evil speaking from outside sources and some inner workings. Daily, our enemies and our foes would watch my going and my coming.

In some cases, we were preyed on by individuals and companies who meant us no good. They worked on my stress level at times, causing me to nearly stumble under pressure, but I always carried with me an ace in the whole and their names were grace, mercy, protector, victor, keeper, mind regulator, hope, peace, joy, steadfastness, and wisdom. No matter what, I never left home without them. No matter what, I kept my head up to the sky where all of my help and deliverance came from; in the words of my beloved Mom, "Thank God for Jesus."

I was reminded through the Word of God in 2 Corinthians 4:8–12, the apostles were great sufferers, yet they met with wonderful support in time. As a believer, by now, I was beginning to fully experience the pain of being forsaken by my so-called friends, as well as persecuted by enemies; but I had to apply my life personal application to the belief that my God will never leave me nor forsake me.

Especially now! There were extreme days of testing and much room for doubting and allowing my fears to completely take over my life from within me, especially when this was considered to be uncharted waters (as it was for me at this time). While experiencing these personal battles, I endured various fighting from without as well as within various sources; yet it was while I was in those battles that I noticed that no matter what, we were not being destroyed but rather progressing by the hand of the Almighty God.

In this same chapter of our lives, it was vital for us to notice that while the apostle spoke of their sufferings as a counterpart (a thing that fits another perfectly) of the sufferings of Christ, they were able to display the fact that people might also see the power of Christ's resurrection being demonstrated in their lives as well. That was our hope that others would see Jesus through our lives in then.

At the end of this book, my greatest accomplishment is that others will know and realize that God is always there for whoever is willing to allow him into their hearts and lives. I want the readers of this book to know that even when they are cast down to be destroyed by Satan and the world, they must remember as born-again believers, they will never be destroyed. They can rest safely and assuredly in the arms of Jesus knowing that he alone will fight every battle if they would just keep still.

Christ alone knows how long the battle should be, how hot the furnace should be, and the purpose of the battle and the consequences of the endurance. Even still, there will be times when persecution seems to pursue us with a vengeance from place to place, desiring to rob us of our God-given joy, peace, and rest. Persecution comes to imprison the people of God to immobilize their purpose in the will of God to threaten us to keep silent to the point of scandalizing our names. But our God never leaves us or forsakes us. Though we are followed close by evil men and left by our friends, we are not forsaken of God.

THE ENEMY COMES TO KILL, STEAL, AND DESTROY!

After a couple of weeks of this woman's presence in our home (although she appeared nice, friendly, concerned, and helpful), I could see the underlings of her intentions. I continued to plead the blood of Jesus over my family's well-being over everything. There were also calls from people, family and otherwise, questioning my overall judgment of Audie's well-being, and perhaps even my intent for his well-being. I never doubted the will of God for our journey not even once.

Their door bell was constantly ringing and people "just happened to be in the neighborhood" or would drop by unannounced, not having a clue when to leave. Our telephone was constantly ringing off the hook. I was diligent in keeping up with the upkeep of the house, both in and out. I was faithful in paying bills, working two jobs, making dinner, washing, and the everyday goings-on of just living. I was stretched without an end in sight. Still, I relied on and leaned on God with every substance of weakness I possessed.

One night after getting up around 3:00 a.m., my feet hitting the floor nonstop, my body felt as though it no longer belonged to me. When I looked in the mirror, I didn't even recognize the person I once knew. The one who always had a bright, vibrant smile, the calm, soothing voice that would pray anyone up under a rock if need be—the warrior who was always ready, swift, and eager to the run to the aid of anyone who needed me in a moment's notice. Nevertheless I learned how to whisper, "Jesus, I trust you."

After a full day's work, I would return home if I was fortunate around 7:00 p.m. or 8:00 p.m. to continue the task at hand. I remembered looking in the mirror. After going passed it, I heard in my spirit say to me, "Stop and take a long look at who you are looking at. Be assured that the enemy is after your mind, and you need to know that there is serious warfare over your mind. Trust in the Lord with all of your heart and lean not unto your own understanding."

I realized instantly that if I was to survive this journey, and I will need to entrust ALL that I was created to be into the mighty hands of my Lord and Savior with absolutely no room for error. I knew that meant that I needed to totally surrender my life unto God like yesterday!

For months, I felt incredibly alone. Not just lonely, but alone. There is a major difference between the two. For me, it was the feeling that no one even knows you are missing or in need of help. It was having the sinking feeling down at the pit of my stomach that vied for my attention between faith and fear, never stopping to remind me of what I was up against and that I may not survive this major blow.

Not only did I feel that I had to contend with daily negative stuff and feedback from various individuals, but I was also dealing with challenges that was nothing short of demonic spirits attacking me from every angle on the job. Thank God I was a good student of prayer and discipline, or there is no way I could have survive it on my own recognizes.

If I didn't know or understand anything else, I fully understood and knew all too well the power, motivation, and will of prayer. It didn't matter whether I felt alone, or if I'd be alone or not. I opened my mouth and began to cry, "Jesus help me!" And I am very happy to report each and every time, he not only showed up, but he showed completely out! Every time I cried out the Lord's name, I believed that I instantly gained strength from on high and new mercy to carry me through another day's journey. I felt taller from the inside out and more assured than ever to continue to move forward, looking unto God for my family's total deliverance.

In the month of December, we did not have a lot of money, although others may have thought how could they have managed all that time? Some believed that there were other entities or agencies who must be involved, such as the veterans association and perhaps the social security. They just didn't know that we were trusting and believing God for our every single need.

Through the resources of others who loved God and desired to do his will in our lives, at various times, they came with services and resources and quietly left them without fanfare or notice, and we appreciated it to the highest. Not realizing it at the time, the individual who was in our home under the pretense of "home health" was anything but. She not only stole personal things from our home every chance she got, but she also stole checks, cash, and every designer purse she could possibly carry from my home—all the while my husband lie just a couple of feet from her unable to get up from his sickbed and fend for himself.

I have to believe that there is a very special place for people like her being reserved for her one day, and unless she repents and seriously change her ways, she is guaranteed to hit her target spot-on. This person, for lack of a better word, not only stole things from me. She took it upon herself to invite her family (son and boyfriend from prison) into our home at a time when we were at one of our earthly lowest points.

I honestly believed that somewhere along the lines, these two individuals conspired to rob us blind and perhaps their intentions where to go beyond that! BUT God built a hedge of protection around my family despite their evil and perverse ways. When I questioned the woman and her accomplice about certain things she had done, she had the nerve to suggest that I was losing it and that I had no earthly idea of what I was talking about at all.

This woman was not only a loose cannon but she was toxic to her core. When I talked to her, I realized that she had no apparent consciousness of remorse or betrayal. She merely existed and operated at a skeletal level and mindset. At best, this woman somehow felt that the things she had stolen from others should have been hers in the first place.

In the days ahead before the dealings between this lunatic and mine ended, I was shown a home video of this woman and her boyfriend cooking breakfast in our kitchen while my husband was shut up in a bedroom in the back without food for his own stomach.

There it was, all on video camera, him pretending to be cooking for a cooking food network and demonstrating for the cameras how he was preparing "my family" food for the vultures who were eagerly partaking of same. They had the nerve to have the music blasting in the background while the two of them laughed it up for the camera. I filed a police report, but was told that I could not do so because I allowed the woman into my home. I replied and told the police while I understood I allowed this woman into my home, to take care of my spouse while I was hard at work, it was never meant to serve as a personal invitation to steal, rob, or abuse my family at will on any day.

It didn't matter to the police. The law was on the criminal's side. This woman had the audacity to show up at our home the very next day at 4:45 a.m., asking me to let her and her boyfriend in so that they could talk and discuss things. She was sure that I was making a horrible mistake and that it was just a misunderstanding even though the items that I knew I had purchased and owned along with checks and money before now were stolen from my house just hours later by her and her accomplice.

Not only was this woman crazy and should never be trusted to work in any one's home or facility, she should spend some serious time behind bars and in a nut house. Did she seriously think that I would once again trust her anywhere near my home and spouse so that this madness could start all over again? Not only did this person believe that I was somehow mistaken about her, but she also brought her boyfriend alone with her to help talk some sense into me to allow her to start all over again.

They continued to call and text me days after this had taken place asking me could they use my name and phone number as a possible job reference for the both of them.

Eventually, the boyfriend asked for forgiveness; however, the girlfriend pretended she had done nothing wrong. I had to pray for help in forgiveness because I was extremely angry, hurt, shocked, and overwhelmed by it all.

To begin with, it took all the resolve within me to allow her into our home in the first place. To trust someone that I didn't even know into my home over my husband and access into our personal, private lives was one of the hardest things I have ever had to do. I prayed daily for God's protective hand over my spouse and myself and that he would keep us safe and when this happened to us, I was hurt beyond measure.

After much prayer for forgiveness in my heart toward the both of them, I realized that for me to move forward and to allow God's choice blessings in my life to continue to flow, I must forgive and do it right away. It was a difficult thing to do when I realized that I was dealing with a psychopath that was curt, foul-mouthed, and possessed no repentance about the wrong she had done at all. I asked God to please help me to let it go and move forward.

Not only did God allow that forgiveness and mercy to flow through me, he also showed me the bigger picture in that episode. One day as I was sitting alone, the Holy Spirit began to say to me, "Even though it cost you greatly, this is what it meant to her."

I was baffled to say the least. The Holy Spirit taught me that the property stolen was in mine that I had paid for those items stolen from me and that this deranged woman had absolutely no right to come into our home, on private property, and take it upon herself for any reason to steal and rob us of whatever she deemed was hers to have.

However, the Holy Spirit further reminded me that concerning all that was at stake—our lives, robbery of the house in its entirety, tampering of the computer, and even possible death at the hands of this nut or someone she could have conspired with to have harm done to us, God had spared both our lives tremendously. That in itself was priceless!

Because of the grace and mercy of God he allowed this woman to take that which she deemed was important and necessary for her at the moment. Perhaps she could have pawned those stolen purses for quick cash. The checks and cash stolen could be disposed of right away in hopes that I would probably never miss it, or when and if I did, she would simply deny the truth.

The bigger and most important picture of them all was that God spared me and Audie's life on earth so that we could continue to be a living and viable testimony to those who would never believe that God was and is still able above all else to keep his many promises toward us even when we are in tight places and treading on dangerous grounds. Faced with imminent dangers or being pursued by the enemy, God is able nonetheless.

After listening to the Holy Spirit minister to me about my then situation, I realized that not only was I still blessed, but that my entire family had remained hidden under the shadow of the Almighty God. And even when the enemy came in, "so shall they fear the name of the Lord from the west, and his glory from the rising of the sun. When the enemy shall come in like a flood, the Spirit of the Lord shall lift up a standard against him" (Isa. 59:19, KJV). In that moment, I realized that I had more reasons in fact to praise God rather than to complain.

I realized that God was allowing me to see that the enemy had been allotted ample amount of time to do what he came to do, and when his time had expired, he was going to be totally removed from our lives, never to return again. Praise God and thank you, Jesus!

Finally, I called her and told her had I only known of her intentions the day that I encountered her in the rehabilitation center I would have never allowed her to come within a thousand feet near my family. I actually felt sorry for this woman who fell so low from a lack of confidence to ask for what she needed rather than to resort to stealing, lying, cheating, scheming, and even becoming delusional into actually believing that the both of us could possibly still become friends. And just forget about everything. I said to her, "We were never friends. You were someone who pretended to come into our home to work, to rob and to steal from us, at the very least, our trust in you to complete a job, did you forget about that?"

Moving forward from that situation, I have been healed, delivered, and set free from that inconvenience and temporary setback because what was designed to destroy and steal our peace eventually made me stronger and lifted me higher in the realm of trust and security in the Lord. Now I realize that we had actually witnessed a wolf in sheep's clothing, in 3D.

We chose to grow from that situation and let God arise and the enemy be scattered. Since that moment, we have had several home health individuals come into our home—all of them promising to meet certain standards that never got measured and/or met because there was always a rhyme or reason why they could not do one thing or the other. This time though, in all instances, we learned that we were more in control of the events happening around us than I had previously given us credit for.

When the workers didn't show up on time, they didn't get paid. When the workers came to work, they had a sign in sheet that documented their time that they were actually in our home.

They were required to list the work that they performed and for how long they were there. If they didn't want to comply, they didn't have to; however, they also were no longer on our watch either. I now understood that if I'd allow people to walk all over me, they would. And they would treat Audie and I like we were victims or helpless people without a God. The devil is a liar and a deceiver too.

WALKING INTO HIS SEASONS

Each time various doctors or administrators would tell me that Audie would not progress beyond a certain point, we would declare differently over him. Not only would Audie surpass their personal judgment, but the Lord would prove the enemy once again wrong. Audie entered the Baylor Institute for Rehabilitation on April 26, 2013 at 7:30 p.m. one way and began thriving ever since. He immediately began to draw others to him by way of his demeanor and humbleness.

Day and night, the doctors, therapists, and nurses would come in and pray over him. Most would cry physically with compassion and empathy not because of his condition but because of his disposition. Audie is a man of prayer, favor, and great faith in the Lord he serves. He trusts and rest in the Lord, recognizing that with God all things are possible to him.

He lives in a state of calmness, meekness, and humbleness. He readily accepts what God allows. One night while at the institute, he was awakened by severe chest pains. His heart rate was dropping when the nurses came in with their machines and pills for him to deter him from possibly having another heart attack. Audie steadily remained calm, and I knew that he was praying as well. This time he began to cry, and at one point, he looked at me and said, "Babe, I don't know how much more my heart can take. I am tired of being in constant pain."

I climbed over in that bed with him and drew him close to me and told him that it was okay. I began to minister to him in song and word, and I told him it's okay to cry and to even show weakness at times because it is when we are at our weakest, our God is strong. Recognizing that he had already been through so much in his life, we still decided to believe God even in our now.

But I didn't want him to give up on himself because I wasn't, and I was sure that there were countless of others praying for him as well. Whatever was happening at the moment, God was with us, and he alone was going to see us through this. Eventually during the early morning hours, Audie was taken to the emergency room, but praise be to God after a battery of tests, they were unable to find anything wrong with him and released him back to the rehab center. I was able to still make it to work on time. I continued to pray in faith, believing that God was working all things out on our behalf.

Audie remained in the rehabilitation from April 26 through May 30, 2013. Then he was released to go home. Prior to that date, the Lord really impressed upon my heart to give him a fiftieth birthday party. But it wasn't just any old birthday celebration. It was a celebration of life birthday party. I threw his party downtown at a place called the T&P Building.

It's an over a hundred years old building that has rich historical meaning. I invited about forty-five people to come. The food was catered, and there was a special guest to play music. Mr. Richmond Punch. Ironically, he had just finished playing the week before for some very significant individuals. The week before that, I was told that he played for Denzel Washington! How blessed were we to have him play for Audie.

To make the celebration even more special, dear friends and family members helped me to make it possible, especially Mr. and Mrs. Kemp. I truly thank God for the both of them. They were extremely supportive and loving. Reggie, Debra, and I did the food tasting, and it was absolutely delicious. The caterers were called Kitchen Caterers. They came highly recommended. Ironically, there were some guests from the church who recognized the caterer, and through their favor with the caterer, we gained favor that night in terms of special perks. We danced, celebrated, laughed, cried, and toasted for the man of the hour—it was nothing short of sweet and compassionated. I thank God for all who attended. After the event, Audie had to return to the rehabilitation center because technically, he was still registered there and wasn't allowed to leave the premises, but the facility made a special exception. Thank God for small favors! Audie had a blast and was grinning from ear to ear. He said, "Babe, I thought we were going to just have cake and ice cream at home."

I said, "Sweetheart, now you know when it comes to you, anything is possible." It was so refreshing to see the look of joy and laughter on his face. I absolutely adore Audie. He is the sunshine in my day.

Shortly after his birthday, he was released after Memorial Day, and he came home. I wasn't quite sure what our next move would be as far as his therapy was concerned, but I was sure that God had a plan in mind. He was home for about a week before we got a call that Audie would be attending outpatient physical therapy at the same location but a different section. We were both extremely excited. One of the guys volunteered to take him to his sessions three times a week. Audie began to flourish there because he felt comfortable with the team, and he was familiar with most of the routine asked of him.

At Baylor Rehabilitation Institute, Audie became more than an ordinary patient, he was more like family. They looked out for him and called him when he was out to see if he was okay. They prayed for his healing daily at the rehab. God was so faithful to us during these turbulent times. And his grace is and was so incredibly amazing.

Through all of my various experiences, the ups and downs, if nothing else, I had learned it was imperative for me to remain focused on what was ahead of me. I recognized that I could never ever make it alone without God at the sole helm of my everyday life. I sought him like a deer panting for its water. I cried out to him at every turn, and I asked him to please go before us and make all of our crooked paths plain. I knew that I could no longer allow any roadside distractions, interruptions, hiccups, sidebars, or just general unnecessary busyness to interrupt my flow in the will and word of God. It was necessary for me to keep it moving.

In September 2013, about 3:00 a.m., for some reason, I was awakened, and the question crossed my mind about what was I going to do. I had tried several different people to come in to our home and help us, and although some were much better than the others service-wise, none of them were what we needed. But I knew that I could no longer afford to continue handling matters in the manner that I currently was, so I began to pray to God to please show me the way through this situation. At about 3:30 a.m., I felt the peace of God over me, so I began to talk with the Lord about leaving Audie alone in the house while I went to work.

While it was scary at first, I recognized that God loved Audie more than I could even fathom because he belonged to God. I knew that God had promoted me to a new post over a year ago, and he would not have given it to me if He did not deem me worthy of it; the mere fact that God did spoke volumes to my life: (1) that he trusted me to be promoted into something higher in which I called it "progress in faith"; (2) now he wanted me to trust Him with Audie, I called it "putting faith into action, which moves the hand of God."

Together Audie and I decided to move forward by putting everything we knew about God into his capable hands alone. We choose not to worry, fret, and doubt or wonder what was going to happen. How it was going to happen or when it might happen. We believed God and moved forward. We made up in our spiritual minds that we were not going to allow anyone else into our home who (1) did not love God with all of their hearts first, (2) loved us secondly, and (3) love what they did for a living. It could not just be about money and a job.

What I discovered was although it takes money to live, money in itself must not become their total motivation to perform a job. While it is understandable that it requires money to live, having a heart and compassion for what one does must fit into the equation somewhere at the top of the list; otherwise, it is just money-motivated and nothing else. I decided we deserved more than that. After all, their well-being was at stake, and to the both of us it was vital that we live in a state of peace and safety no matter what.

Daily we prayed together before deciding to leave Audie at home alone without any one being there with him. We started off our day with prayer. I would prepare his medicine, make breakfast and always prayed over him before leaving. Sometimes I would return home within several hours to share lunch together before heading back to work.

Prior to the change, a typical day included getting up at 4:00 a.m. or 5:00 a.m., preparing breakfast, preparing medications, getting Audie ready to go to therapy, dropping him off before heading off to work, working for three hours, returning to pick him up from therapy, driving him home to prepare lunch, and then going back to work and working late before heading home to prepare dinner.

About two weeks after making this decision, I felt my body shift into tiredness. I cried out to the Lord for help. I felt as though I just needed a mental, physical, and spiritual break from it all. I was unsure whether or not anyone outside of my personal physical and spiritual scope could comprehend the strain that I had been under for years, which has only been heightened through this situation.

However, I realized today that I had to get help in order to compete; however, not just any help but specific help. Daily I continuously cried out to the Lord in asking him for his guidance and direction for our lives. I love God with all of my heart and mind but most importantly I know that God loves us and that pleased my heart more.

AN ANSWERED PRAYER

Within a couple of days, I received a text from a church member who just happened to send me a message inquiring how Audie and I were doing. She said that we had been on her mind for a while, and she just wanted to double check and make sure that we were okay. After probing for a bit, I finally decided to tell her what had happened a week ago with Audie's seizure and hospitalization. She sounded quite concerned and asked what she and others could do because there were others who loved us and prayed for us all the time. She went on to say how I should allow others to help me and not be so private and push people away.

Perhaps on the outside, I can understand why others may see it as me pushing others away or being private and unassuming; however, I saw and knew it to be differently. Sometimes it is much easier for me just to do it myself or to pray about it and allow God to send the right person(s) into our path than to tell a bunch of people all of our business and needs, who may start off being concerned and end up spreading what they do not know or fully understand in the local marketplace or streets.

In the end, the only thing I received from it all was being delayed and detained. Not only was it a waste of my time, but it can also be viewed as more unnecessary interruptions from things that I have to take care of in moving forward.

Don't get me wrong, I loved and appreciated everyone who was sincere about assisting us; however, I absolutely had zero tolerance for those who came, saw, and twisted everything around.

They were some who showed up and appeared to be more interested in what they heard as opposed to what God was doing. Still to me, there was absolutely no room in our lives for haters, investigators, or simply deal breakers.

We chose to keep it moving. I believe if you want to be a blessing to someone, and then do so, and God will reward you. If you don't want to a blessing, there is no need to pretend to be something or do something that you are going to become frustrated or irritated about later. There is a big difference when someone does something from the heart and when it is just for show. When flesh is involved, it does not last very long, and the flesh will often let you know how they feel sooner rather than later. Let me correct that, they will let you know and everyone else as well.

This person who called me is a sweet individual who I have no doubt that she loves God and even us however, the timing of her desire was not the will of God for what she personally stated that she wanted to do for us. The truth of the matter would later be revealed in a follow-up text within a week from her. We understood and very much appreciated her efforts and concerns, however; we chose to be still and wait upon God for our answer.

In the meantime, Labor Day was fast approaching, and Audie and I were getting excited. My sister and nephew from Memphis were going to be driving up for the weekend, but they had car problems and were not able to make it. While they we saddened by the fact that they were not going to be able to make it, we were happy that they didn't get stranded on the highway trying to get to Texas. God is good in his protection over his children.

Wednesday night leading up to Labor Day, I texted my goddaughter in San Antonio, Texas to see if they were still going to make it. To my surprise, not only were they planning on coming, but her mom, kids, and her husband also were coming. They were going to be leaving Friday night after work. They arrived safely around 12:30 a.m. We were really happy to see them. It was refreshing. We all sat up and talked for about thirty to forty-five minutes once they arrived.

The next morning, I picked up my sister and brother-in-law from Detroit who were coming in at 10:30 a.m. as well. I was too excited to see the both of them and could not wait to pick them up. My goddaughter and I arrived at the airport just as they were waiting outside. The day was shaping up just wonderfully. Brenda must admit nothing prepared her for what was about to take place and perhaps cause a shift experience to enter into their lives.

Once we arrived back at home, everyone hit it off smoothly; no one was standoffish, shy, or pretentious. In fact, it almost seemed as though everyone had known each other for years when in fact they had just met for the very first time. We laughed, ate, laughed some more, and even ate twice as much. Everyone chipped in and supported one another in whatever cause.

My goddaughter and mother cooked as if they were cooking for a small army on all the days that they were there. Her godson fixed and restored everything that was not nailed down. He even mowed the front and back lawn. I just love him! Even the kiddos got in on some exercise by taking out the trash, washing dishes, or whatever was necessary.

During our time together, my brother-in-law and sister was just an absolute godsend. They were encouraging, motivating, supportive, and a shoulder to lean on. My brother-in-law provided strength and support for Audie, and even devoted some time to work with him in his therapy. Audie was delighted and looked forward to the time they spent together. At some point during one of the days that they were together, my brother-in-law said to me that he wanted to talk with the both of us about something that had been on his mind but wanted to run it by me first.

He said that when my sister Dorothy retired in December, they would like to come back to Texas and dedicate about thirty to forty-five days of their time in helping us out around the house.

I almost fainted. It was just out of the blue and one of those suddenly blessings. Ironically, just a week prior, I had just talked to God about this very subject matter and here it is right in front of my face, the blessing appeared.

These are people who I knew loved God and loved us to. Their intentions were to bless us and not to harm us in any way. Not wanting to totally freak out my brother-in-law, I was a little restrained in my response and careful not to allow myself to break out into an all-out praise and worship session without any warning which may or may not have literally scared him.

Even though I was too excited about the news, I wasn't too sure about getting my hopes too high. I waited to see if he would bring up the subject again, and guess what, he did. Not just once, but several times. When I looked into his eyes, I could sense and feel his sincerity about assisting us. Because I am not one who readily asks for help not because of pride, but because I like to try all I can to do what I can before asking others so when I do come to someone for help, they will know that I have exhausted all applicable measures in the process.

On Sunday night, as everyone was cleaning up the kitchen, I decided to check in on Audie to see how he was doing. When I did, he began to cry because he wanted so badly to be in the group with everyone else, but at the moment, he was not able to do so. When I saw the sadness in his eyes, the first thing that I said was, "The devil is a liar, and he will not steal, borrow, lease, rent, or take our joy."

I called in the troops, and they gathered around Audie's bed and began to pray, intercede, lament, and cry out to the Lord on Audie's behalf. In the process of it all, I felt the shift of God move in the midst of the atmosphere. During our prayer, praise, and worship time together, the tears fell. But the troops kept on praying, shouting, and worshipping in the midst of it all.

After a while, Audie began to lift up his hands and his voice and cry out to God for himself. He is determined to get up and walk and to recover fully. The Lord has shown me on two different occasions him doing so, and I and the others believed the report of the Lord. Everyone reported the next day of how well they slept the rest of that night. They knew that the presence of the Lord had visited us and we were definitely in his presence.

Each time I looked at my husband, I could sense that God was doing something mighty in his being. His countenance looked differently daily. His demeanor was more assured and affirmed. His tone was firm and steadfast. He knows that God loves him—no doubt about it. We all agreed daily that God was more than enough and all that we needed. We agreed that by his strife, Audie was healed. We agreed that he will walk again and that his health will be fully be restored and renewed in Jesus's name.

After a couple of hours of allowing this good news to process, then came my sister with the same information. I remembered looking at her and thinking, God can this possibly be your will for right now in our lives? Is this my answered prayer? I continued to think what an unselfish, loving gift for someone to give of themselves to another human being as to become a servant not just to me and Audie but also unto God. To know my sister is to know one of God's genuine servants. She walks it and talks it, and it is evident by her conversations that God reins in her life.

After my extended family from San Antonio had returned home on Monday, Dorothy and Otis remained in our home until Thursday morning. In the meantime, our time shared together was nothing short of priceless and anointed. Otis took great pain in making sure that the cars were up to par before leaving. He had the oil changed, the tires checked, the alignment completed, and the next thing on the list was the struts.

He shared with me personal things about his medical condition and how God had delivered him and brought him out. Otis felt ready and able to provide that same type of compassion and support to others. I was so overjoyed and happy. I could not wait to see what God was up to and how he was going to turn this situation around for our good!

In the days since everyone has returned home, I continued to feel such a deep closeness to the Lord. I knew somewhere there were others praying and interceding for us with a genuine heart, soul, and purpose. I could sense it. Audie and I were in a different place as we were continuously moving forward.

On Sunday, September 8, 2013, our bishop preached about the sound of faith using the book of Hebrews. One of the valuable lessons that I walked away from that service with was that I lived in a state of readiness. My faith is activated by my now attitude toward the obstacle, situation, circumstance, or problem.

I believe that God is able to handle all of my current situations and that nothing surprises him. Nothing gets past his approval. Nothing can stop him from blessing me and my family. And nothing and no one can stay his hand when it comes to blessing us. At the end of the day, I am grateful that he loves me and I am feeling the love.

HEARING HIS VOICE

The Baylor Rehabilitation Institution had been a wonderful safe haven for Audie's weekly therapy. But like anything else in life, all good things must come to an end at some point. I was told toward the end of August that Audie's therapy would be ending soon and that he would have to look for another place of in-home home health to come in to assist him. The rehabilitation workers looked very intense when they thought that we didn't have plan in mind, and I was asked constantly about what I was going to do moving forward. Always my first and last response would be, "Trust in the Lord."

They looked worried and expected me to already have all the answers, which I didn't have. I decided not to worry but to truly cast every care upon the Lord believing that he cared for me and our situation.

One night after getting home from work and everything had been taken care at the rehab; I went to bed and began to talk to God about our situation. I asked God what I should do regarding Audie's therapy and daily care. I also poured my heart out to God about my not wanting to allow someone else in our home alone with Audie while I was away at work. More importantly, I did not want someone who would literally assume that they would have total free reign over my spouse and my home.

I no longer felt comfortable or remotely at peace with a total stranger having access to us whether I was home or not. So I needed wisdom like never before, so I leaned in hard on God for answers. I said, "Lord, the next person that will take care of Audie while I am away must first and foremost love You, love Audie, and love doing home healthcare as a ministry." I was just unwilling to take anything less.

After making my petition known unto the Lord, this is the response that I received within a couple of days. The date was August 23, 2013.

Entrust your loved ones to me; release them into my protective care. They are much safer with Me than in your clinging hands. If you let a loved one become an idol in your heart, you endanger that one—as well as yourself.

Remember the extreme measures I used with Abraham and Isaac. I took Isaac to the very point of death to free Abraham from son worship. Both Abraham and Isaac suffered terribly because of the father's undisciplined emotions. I detest idolatry, even in the form of parental love.

When you release loved ones to me, you are free to cling to my hand. As you entrust others into my care, I am free to shower blessings on them. My presence will go with them wherever they go, and I will give them rest. This same presence stays with you, as you relax and place your trust in me. Watch to see what I will do. (Gen. 22:9–12, Eph. 3:20, Exod. 33:14)

From that very moment forward, I did not look back, nor regret my decision in entrusting Audie entirely unto the Lord. To me, that was the answer that I was looking for and needed. Why not entrust him to the one who obviously loves him more, I thought. Christ is not only our Redeemer, Savior, healer, fortress, provider, and our all in all amongst other obvious things, but he is the creator of all things, including Audie. No one on this planet loves him more than that—although I would make a strong second even if I said so myself.

Since the week of Labor Day 2013, I have not asked anyone or hired anyone to come and work and/or stay at our home during the day to be with Audie while I am at work. I have witnessed him both physically and spiritually become more strengthened every day. I was more determined than ever before to move forward and make great strides. He is much more alert, disciplined in his healing process, and determined to receive his blessings daily from the Lord.

I felt as though I had to learn a more valuable lesson in trusting and taking God at his word when I first hear him speak to me. When I ask God for specifics, I needed to believe in that same moment that I would receive exactly what I have asked for.

Audie told me, "Babe, unless I call you and tell you that I need you to come home, stay at work and make sure you have a blessed day. And don't forget to eat your lunch." I am still laughing and basting in the blessings of God on that note.

Daily, I sing God's blessings and praising in knowing that our God is nothing less than awesome! He alone makes all things new! Every day, my faith walk with God intensified. I realized that my faith required us to trust him even when we could not see the obvious that is he alone was taking care of everything for us whether we realized it or not. So it stands to reasoning that we would only apply our personal faith and trust in God to action instead of praying and continuing to worry all at the same time.

Daily when I did my personal due diligence at home by making Audie breakfast, giving him his daily medications, securing the house, and heading off to work, I did so in complete confidence and assurance that God was with the both of us and that absolutely no weapon that was formed against us shall prosper. When I returned home, I was not disappointed or surprised that God had kept his word.

This has made me stronger in the Lord and more assured that not only is God a keeper of his Word, but he is the author and the finisher our souls. I am making a conscious effort to stop worrying about anything that I have no control or authority over, which is just about anything that is spiritually important.

The enemy would love nothing more than for me to stress out about everything and quit my job, become a prisoner in my own home, stop living, and put my head in the sand. I know all too well that God is and has always been in control, and he is definitely in charge of our lives.

When one stresses over things, it sends a message that everything is becoming undone. That people are not in control of their emotions, surroundings, situations, or their actions at times. At times, as a people, we may experience the feeling or the notion that our whole world is crumbling before our eyes. Then panic sets in, and if we are not careful, the spirit of defeat takes over, and for sure we are a goner. As long as we continue to respond to our fleshly emotions, we will truly sink.

I realize that all too often, stress brings about unexpected anxiety. When that takes place on the inside, it releases "turmoil and fear which causes us to never be still," just like Job (Job 30:27). We may call it affliction, anxiety, or tension when it is happening to us. However, it could quite possibly be physically related to the symptoms of a stressful headache, again deriving from things we are refusing to let go and allow God to handle and take care for us in the first place.

While we maintain that we just want to be happy and live a peaceful uneventful life, we even dream of days and times when our lives will be stress-free, forgetting that to reap those benefits, we must get into position to do so. We must be careful to not read the scriptures and quote the verses, but we must live them out loud! The Bible has many helpful scriptures for dealing with stress. I would like for my readers to meditate upon this verse when they are feeling stressed out:

Peace I leave with you; my peace I give to you. Not as the world gives do I give to you. Let not your hearts be troubled, neither let them be afraid. (John 14:27) There is something to be said about resting in the peace of God. Not only does it provide a sense of solace when we do, it also says a lot about how we personally view God and what he personally means to us individually.

Believe it or not, our God is closer to us than the very breath we breathe. We must learn how to practice recognizing his presence being near us. Sometimes we are so busy worrying and fretting over any and every little thing, we cannot bask in his intimate presence.

For the most part, some may feel unless they are "in a church" by sitting in their favorite pew at a certain time, doing the same old thing, behaving in the same old manner. However, they are not carrying out the will of God for their lives, let alone resting and/or being at peace with God. All the while, what God only truly wants from us is to know and experience him intimately.

If we could get to know our God's presence, we would never experience another day of loneliness or feel that we are lonely again why you ask? Because we understand that our Father already knows every thought we possess—the ones that have been released and those that have yet to be uttered.

Because God is a great God as human beings, we have a tendency to fear him in the wrong way because just the thought of being near God terrifies them. The first thing that most people think of is, "I'm not good enough. I'm not saved," or "God is going to punish me." We try to hide our sins, thoughts, actions, or even our emotions from the very one we should be running to because he made us and fully understands us. Even our very tears are a language unto the Lord. While we can easily deceive mankind, we can never, ever deceive God at any time.

God wants us to know that his own children know him. The ones who have surrendered their lives over to Jesus Christ—those who have been cleansed through the blood of Jesus and those that the Father has clothed in his righteousness—recognize that they are blessed by his nearness. We have absolutely nothing at all to fear, stress, or worry about.

In fact, the Isaiah 40:30–31, it reads, "Even youths shall faint and be weary, and young men shall fall exhausted; but they who wait for the Lord shall renew their strength; they shall mount up with wings like eagles; they shall run and not be weary; they shall walk and not faint." Also, Philippians 4:6–7 reminds us, "Do not be anxious about anything, but in everything by prayer and supplication with thanksgiving let your requests be made known to God. And the peace of God, which surpasses all understanding, will guard your hearts and your minds in Christ Jesus."

This is and will continue to be a fresh season in our lives whereby I am learning to walk by a different drum beat and not my own strength. I felt renewed, refreshed, enlightened, and fortified in Christ Jesus. I am a living testament that I can do all things through, Christ which strengthens me and like Peter. "Humble yourselves, therefore, under the mighty hand of God so that at the proper time he may exalt you, casting all your anxieties on him, because he cares for you" (1 Peter 5:6–7)

I am content in knowing now that no matter what comes our way, Audie and I will always know that God alone will see us through. We are definitely committed to God and each other, and our focus is on what really matters most in life. We have both found out it is not about what we possess in life but who we have a hidden treasure in. It is not about our zip code but where our eternal status will end.

It is not about our wealth or the lack thereof because we know that our Father is rich both in houses and land, and he keeps on making ways out of no way. The fact that he will never leave us or forsake us more than makes up the difference in everything that we think we need.

Together, we realize that we are in the center of his will and purpose, and right there is where we long to be. In fact, it is safe to go on record in saying that we are purpose-driven because of his will for our lives. We have come this far by faith and not by sight. Even during some of our most challenging, bleak, and very dark days when we were at our absolute lowest points, we thought that we would break and drop from the point of exhaustion we still called him Lord over everything.

When distraction, disappointment, rejection, fear, doubt, and even setups were coming at us from seemingly every direction we humbled ourselves before the Almighty King and said even now, "Lord, thy will be done in our lives." There were days I was told by others that I would not make it through and that it would be impossible for me to handle it all, it was the Word of God that came to comfort and to surround me and lead me through my personal journey one minute at a time.

At the outset of it all I remember there were many nights while sleeping on a hard cot, in a smelly hospital room surrounded by bleak walls, hospital equipment, nurses entering the room at all times turning on the overhead bright lights, it was a true nightmare. Those were times when I first told myself this is just a bad nightmare and that I would wake up soon and get a big laugh out of it, only to find out that this was anything but, and that this was just the beginning of a new temporary chapter in my journey.

I remember trying to scream, but no sound came out. I tried to cry, but there were little time for tears. I wanted to run away and hide, but God steadied me and ordered my foot-steps. When I looked desperately for someone to talk to share my burdens with, I found a soft, safe, and sound place in the arms of my beloved Savior who comforted me without fail. On the days when it would seem that the pain was insurmountable, my heavenly daddy spoke softly in my ear: "Brenda, don't worry." All was indeed well.

Sometimes in the wee hours of the morning when the finances weren't adding up and the bills kept piling up, phone calls poured in from unsuspecting bill collectors demanding this and that, I was reminded of a quote by Watchman Nee: "An unpeaceful mind cannot operate normally. Hence the Apostle teaches us to 'have no anxiety [stress] about anything' (Phil. 4:6). Deliver all anxious thoughts to God as soon as they arise. Let the peace of God maintain your heart and mind (v. 7)." It was then and there that I had my own epiphany in the Word of God.

"When [I, Brenda Murphy] pass through the rivers, they will not sweep over [me]. When [Brenda Murphy] walk through the fire, [she] will not be burned; the flames will not set [her] ablaze" (Isa. 43:2, NIV). That is when I softly called His name and He reminded me of his faithfulness.

That was the very minute that I decided that I was no longer bound and held hostage by the world's standards, thoughts, perceptions, opinions, ideas, concepts, definition or points of views that once held me captive. In that moment, I knew for the first time in my life that I was indeed free to soar as high as I wanted to go in Christ. Only I could believe that he was able to bring me and my family out and that there would be no limits and no boundaries but only increases all around us.

For the first time in my adult life, I was no longer afraid to dream bigger and think outside the box because now I knew all too well who held my real future and that I was predestined to accomplish great things.

I was also reminded that "in almost everything that touches our everyday life on earth; God is pleased when we're pleased. He wills that we be as free as birds to soar and sing our maker's praise without anxiety [stress]." (A. W. Tozer.)

In conclusion of this book, I echo the sentiments of the eloquent writings of Mr. Rick Warren when he wrote the following: "Since God intends to make you like Jesus, he will take you through the same experiences Jesus went through. That includes loneliness, temptation, stress, criticism, rejection, and many other problems."

CROSS-REFERENCES

Isaiah 43:2 — S Isa. 8:7
Isaiah 43:2 — S Ge. 26:3: S Ex. 14:22
Isaiah 43:2 — Isa. 29:6; 30:27
Isaiah 43:2 — Ps. 66:12; Da. 3:25–27